BE RECOGNIZED

*The AI Authority Engine for Experts
Who Want to Be Known,
Be Profitable, and Be Published*

BY
MELANIE JOHNSON
& JENN FOSTER

Be Recognized
The AI Authority Engine for Experts Who Want to Be Known, Be Profitable, and Be Published

JOHNSON, MELANIE, Author
FOSTER, JENN, Author
BE RECOGNIZED
MELANIE JOHNSON, JENN FOSTER

Published by:
ELITE ONLINE PUBLISHING
63 East 11400 South
Suite #230
Sandy, UT 84070
EliteOnlinePublishing.com

ISBN 978-1-961801-92-9 (eBook)
ISBN 978-1-961801-93-6 (Paperback)
ISBN 978-1-961801-94-3 (Hardcover)
ISBN 978-1-961801-95-0 (Audiobook)
LCCN: 2025920703

BUS071000
BUS020000
COM004000

QUANTITY PURCHASES: Schools, companies, professional groups, clubs, and other organizations may qualify for special terms when ordering quantities of this title. For information, email info@eliteonlinepublishing.com.

TABLE OF CONTENTS

BONUS

Before you dive in, we've got something special just for you. We've put together a powerful set of tools and resources to help you get the most out of this book and they're totally free. Just scan the QR code or visit BeRecognized.us/book to grab your bonuses. You'll get our AI Prompt Toolkit, a curated list of Custom GPT's to use for your business, and a go-to AI App Favorites List to save you hours of guesswork. Think of it as your starter pack for becoming unstoppable.

BeRecognized.us/book

PRAISES FOR MELANIE JOHNSON & JENN FOSTER

"Even the most confident entrepreneur will get rattled when they realize the cost of their invisibility. Melanie and Jenn give you the blueprints to Be Recognized. Don't let another day go by without embracing their successful formula."

—Sam Malone, President of 5/12 New Media

"A great and mandatory guide by two experts in the industry. Melanie and Jenn not only publish their authors, but they also teach them the industry... There is a huge difference, I discovered. This provides direction and methods necessary to be a successful author in today's fast-paced and evolving literature industry. If you are serious about building your platform and brand, this is a necessary tool."

—Reggie Gray,
President of the International Chamber of Commerce

"Be Recognized is the playbook for leaders who refuse to be invisible in the age of AI. Melanie Johnson and Jenn Foster cut through the noise with a clear, actionable path to dominate your niche, automate growth, and rise as the undeniable authority in your field. This book is not theory, it's execution. From building an AI-powered content engine to turning a single book into a lead-generating empire, every strategy is designed to create momentum and measurable results. If you want to lead, profit, and leave a mark, this is the blueprint you've been waiting for."

—Mark Churella Chairman & CEO
of FDI Group and Hall of Fame Collegiate Wrestler

"Reading Be Recognized was such an inspiring and practical experience for me. Melanie Johnson and Jenn Foster have created a roadmap that makes the process of being seen, heard, and published feel both achievable and exciting. What I truly appreciated is how approachable their strategies are; everything is broken down into clear, actionable steps. I walked away feeling more confident about how to share my story, expand my presence, and position myself as an authority in my field. For me, this book is more than a guide—it's a catalyst. It reminded me that the tools are already within us to be recognized, profitable, and impactful; we just need the right framework to bring it all together. I highly recommend Be Recognized to entrepreneurs, leaders, and anyone ready to elevate their voice and their brand."

—Karen Ballou,
Founder of Immunocologie

FOREWORD

If you told me ten years ago that my mom would write a book teaching entrepreneurs how to dominate the digital world with AI, I probably would've said, "Yeah, that sounds about right." And I would've been half kidding, half terrified.

Because if there's one thing I know about Melanie Johnson, it's that she doesn't wait around for permission, trends, or the 'perfect time.' She sees what's coming, and she *builds* it. Fast. Boldly. And usually with a whiteboard, a bold vision, and at least two dozen browser tabs open.

I've had the unique experience of growing up not just with a mom, but with a mentor, a visionary, and a builder who refused to let life, or the market, define her. After the 2009 crash flipped her world upside down, she didn't fold. She pivoted. Reinvented. Took everything she knew from running multi-million dollar media companies and turned it into a publishing powerhouse. She didn't just bounce back; she bounced *up*. And then she taught other people how to do it too.

As a founder and CEO of my own media company, Clipr, I've seen firsthand how critical visibility, content, and authority are in today's AI-driven world. You can't afford to be the best-kept secret anymore. And that's exactly what this book is about: becoming *the one* who's seen, heard, and remembered.

But here's the best part: this book isn't just written by Melanie. It's powered by the unstoppable force that is Melanie *and* Jenn Foster, a dynamic duo who've helped thousands of authors, speakers, consultants, and business leaders transform their message into a movement. They're both single moms. Both entrepreneurs. Both relentless in their belief that your story matters and your expertise deserves a platform.

You'll learn how to write the book, sure. But more importantly, you'll learn how to *own* your voice, leverage your content, and build an AI-powered authority engine that works for you while you sleep. You'll learn how to stop chasing clients and start magnetizing them. And you'll laugh while you do it, because this book doesn't pull punches, and neither do the women who wrote it.

I grew up watching my mom work crazy hours, run two TV stations, deal with real estate drama, build businesses from the ground up, and still show up to school plays, baseball games, and give me advice I'd pretend not to need. She always taught me that we don't wait to be chosen—we *choose* ourselves. And watching Jenn build her business alongside her kids, yeah, same energy.

So if you're holding this book, just know this: you're about to get handed the keys to visibility, credibility, and scalability. Don't just read it, *use* it.

Because in the age of AI, the only thing more powerful than your content… is your *clarity*.

Let's go build something legendary.

— **Nathan Johnson**
Founder & CEO, Clipr Media
@NathanJohnson

THE NEW AGE OF PUBLISHING MEETS THE NEW AGE OF BUSINESS

The future belongs to those who see possibilities before they become obvious.

- John Sculley

Hey there, Melanie Johnson here, and I'm so excited you've picked up this book!

Let me start with a story that happened just a few months ago. I spoke at our Houston Entrepreneurs meeting in April 2025, surrounded by some of the most brilliant minds I know, including successful business owners, innovative consultants, and industry experts. However, as we began discussing Artificial Intelligence, something fascinating occurred. These incredibly accomplished people, who had built million-dollar businesses and transformed entire industries, suddenly looked like deer in headlights.

"I haven't even played with it yet," one successful consultant admitted. "It feels so overwhelming," said a CEO who runs a multi-million-dollar company. "I know I should be doing something with AI, but I don't know where to start," confessed a business coach who helps others scale their operations.

And in that moment, I realized something profound: we're witnessing the most significant business transformation since the internet, maybe even bigger, and most entrepreneurs are sitting on the sidelines, watching it happen instead of leading it.

Why We Wrote This Book

My business partner, Jenn Foster, and I have been in the publishing world for over ten years. During that time, we've published over 3,000 books and helped countless authors become bestsellers. We've seen firsthand how a well-crafted book can transform a business, establish authority, and create opportunities that seemed impossible just months before.

But here's what we've learned: publishing a book was always just the beginning. The real magic happened when our authors used their books as leverage to build their platforms, scale their businesses, and position themselves as the go-to authorities in their fields.

Now, with AI, that magic has been supercharged beyond anything we ever imagined. We're living in what I call the "New Age of Publishing," meeting the "New Age of Business." For the first time in history, you can write, publish, and promote a bestselling book using AI tools that work faster, smarter, and more effectively than traditional methods. And that book? It becomes the foundation for an AI-powered business system that works 24/7 to build your authority, attract your ideal clients, and scale your impact.

The Speed of Change is Brutal

Remember when the internet came along? Some people called it a fad. My own mom was skeptical, thinking it would never last. We had time to adjust, time to learn, time to ease into this new digital world.

AI isn't giving us that luxury.

This transformation is happening "fast and furious," as we were saying in our Houston group. Every industry is being reshaped at an accelerating pace. The speed is brutal. And here's the hard truth: 90% of business owners are completely unprepared.

Not because they're not smart, they absolutely are. But because they're still playing by the old rules.

The old rules said, 'Work harder.' Put in more hours. Hustle your way to success.

The new rules say: **Work smarter. Build systems. Use leverage.**

And AI is the most powerful leverage multiplier of our lifetime.

The Winners Are Already Being Decided

Here's what we know for certain: The winners in this new era will not be the ones with the most experience in their field. They'll be the ones with the most leverage. The ones who figure out how to use AI not just as a tool, but as a strategic partner that amplifies their expertise, scales their reach, and accelerates their growth.

I'm not talking about using ChatGPT to write a few blog posts or having AI help you with your emails (though we'll cover that too). This is about something far more transformational:

> **Reinventing how you position yourself, how you sell, how you scale, and how you dominate your category.**

It's about becoming the architect of systems that work for you, instead of being the operator who works in them.

What Makes This Book Different

Over the past few years, Jenn and I have been completely immersed in this new world. We've helped experts write books quickly using AI.

We've launched offers using AI tools that traditional methods could never match. We've built automated content machines that position our authors as thought leaders while they sleep. And we've helped entrepreneurs transform from being invisible to industry leaders in under 90 days.

This book is the blueprint behind those transformations.

What you'll find here isn't theory, it's execution. It's not about what might be possible someday; it's about what's working right now. Every strategy, every tool, every framework in this book has been tested in the real world with real businesses achieving real results.

Who This Book Is For

This is your battle plan if you're:

- An entrepreneur who knows your expertise could change lives, but you're struggling to get the right people to notice
- A consultant or coach who's tired of trading time for money and ready to scale your impact
- A business owner who feels like they're always one step behind the competition
- An expert in your field who knows you should be writing a book but feels overwhelmed by the process
- A leader who understands that AI will reshape your industry and wants to be the one doing the reshaping

Most importantly, this book is for people who refuse to be disrupted by artificial intelligence and instead intend to own it, bend it to their will, and use it to scale beyond what they ever thought possible.

What You'll Learn

Throughout these pages, you'll discover:

How to write and publish a bestselling book quickly using AI tools that make the process faster, easier, and more effective than traditional publishing.

The **"Silent Salesperson" strategy** turns your book into a 24/7 lead generation and sales system.

Stage-by-stage AI integration that transforms you from a manual operator into a strategic architect.

The **Frictionless Firm method** for automating your sales and customer communication without losing the human touch.

Authority positioning tactics that establish you as the go-to expert in your field.

Scaling strategies that multiply your impact without multiplying your hours.

Real case studies from entrepreneurs who've used these exact methods to transform their businesses.

The Three Stages of AI Mastery

Throughout this book, we'll take you through what we call the Three Stages of AI Integration:

Stage 1: Automate - Where you use AI to do what you already do, just faster and more efficiently.

Stage 2: Augment - Where AI becomes your business partner, expanding what's possible and creating new revenue streams.

Stage 3: Amplify - Where you build AI-powered systems
that scale your expertise and impact exponentially.

Most business owners get stuck in Stage 1, using AI like a fancy
calculator. The entrepreneurs who will dominate the next decade are
the ones who reach Stage 3, where AI becomes the engine that powers
their entire business ecosystem.

The Time to Act is Now

I won't sugarcoat this: the window for competitive advantage is closing
fast. Every day you wait, your competitors are getting further ahead.
Every month you delay, the gap becomes harder to close.

But here's the good news: if you start now and commit to this journey,
you can leapfrog competitors who have been in business longer, who
have bigger teams, or who have more traditional resources.

Why? Because AI is the great equalizer. It gives small businesses the
tools that only enterprise companies could afford before. It gives
individual experts the reach that only major media companies could
achieve. It gives entrepreneurs the scaling power that only venture-
backed startups could access.

Your Invitation to Lead

The old game is dying. The game where success meant working 80-hour
weeks, where scaling meant hiring more people, and where authority
meant paying your dues for decades.

You get to write the new rules.

The new rules where systems work for you. Where your expertise
reaches thousands instead of dozens. Where your book becomes your
most powerful marketing asset. Where AI amplifies your natural talents
instead of replacing them.

So write those new rules loud. Publish them boldly. And get paid like the leader you are.

This book is your roadmap. These strategies are your weapons. And this moment, right now, is your time to choose.

Will the AI revolution disrupt you, or will you lead it?

The choice is yours. Let's get started.

Ready to transform your business with AI? Let's dive into chapter one and discover how to position yourself as the authority your industry needs.

PART I

THE FOUNDATION
OF AUTHORITY

CHAPTER 1

VISIBILITY IS THE NEW AUTHORITY

It doesn't matter how brilliant you are if no one knows you exist.

–Melanie Johnson

A few years ago, I had a front-row seat to something that changed my entire perspective on what it really means to be seen, and what happens when you're not.

I was working with two entrepreneurs at the same time. Let's call them Angela and Brooke. Both were incredibly smart. Both had decades of experience. Both had real results behind them, transformational client wins, powerful frameworks, speaking experience, the works.

But here's what happened: Angela published a book. She committed to documenting her process, telling her story, and stepping into the public eye with intention. Her message became magnetic. She started getting booked on podcasts, was asked to speak at events, and was suddenly "discovered" by people who had been in her orbit for years but had never noticed her before. She wasn't pitching anymore. People were inviting her.

Brooke didn't publish. She said, "I'll wait until I have more time." She kept showing up, but quietly. A post here, a comment there. No core asset. No clear positioning. Her work stayed invisible, even though it was amazing. A year later, she told me, "I feel like I'm constantly chasing opportunities that I know I deserve."

And that's when it hit me, hard: In today's world, the difference between being booked out and burned out isn't expertise. It's visibility. And not just any visibility, the kind that's anchored in authority.

That moment made me realize that far too many brilliant people are losing in business, not because they're not good enough, but because they're still operating under an outdated belief system:

> "If I work hard enough, someone will notice."

Let me lovingly tell you the truth: **No one is coming to discover you.** If you don't publish your brilliance, position your message, and plant your flag, **you will remain invisible**, even to the people who need you most. The people who rise are the ones who are willing to be recognized.

The New Rules of the Game

It was a Tuesday morning when I saw it happen. I was sipping coffee, scrolling LinkedIn, and there it was, yet another viral post by someone I knew personally. A bright, energetic entrepreneur who had been in business for less than two years. She was sharp, sure, but not wildly experienced. Yet her post had thousands of likes. She was quoted in Forbes that week. She was getting invited to speak at events. And what was her secret? She had a message, she had a method, and she had a book. Most importantly, **she had mastered the modern game of visibility.**

That was the moment I realized:

> We are no longer in the era of "do great work and get discovered."

That era is over.

We've entered a new era. It's **fast**. It's **loud**. It's **algorithm-driven**. And it is absolutely **not slowing down**.

You're not just building a business anymore. You're building a signal. A digital beacon. A data trail that tells both people and machines **who you are, what you do, and whether they should trust you.**

In this world, the brands, businesses, and individuals who win are not necessarily the most talented. They're the most **recognizable**.

Let me say this clearly:

Visibility is the new authority.

And authority is the new leverage.

It's no longer enough to be an expert. Now, you have to be **positioned** as one, *by both people and platforms*. Here's the hard truth: The world is no longer looking for the most qualified person. It's following the most **visible** person who sounds like they know what they're doing.

It's the consultant with a clear message **and a book**. The speaker with a strong framework and an AI-driven content engine. The coach who shows up with confidence, consistency, and conviction.

That shift can feel disorienting. You might think, *"But I've been doing this for 15 years. I've paid my dues. Doesn't that matter?"*

It matters, but not the way it used to, because the new game is about *perception before proof—reputation before resume. Signal before skillset.* That might sound terrifying. But it should also feel incredibly **freeing**. Because here's what it means:

You don't have to be everywhere. You just have to **show up like the expert you already are.** You have to **own your message**, **publish your**

thinking, and build a platform that works for you 24/7, even when you're offline, in a mastermind, or on vacation.

You have to stop hoping the world finds you and start building the ecosystem that positions you **as the one to see.** Welcome to the new rules of the game. Let's make them work in your favor.

Real Talk: What It's Costing You to Stay Invisible

Let's stop soft-pedaling this. The cost of invisibility? It's not just money. It's not just missed leads or lost clients. It's the **erosion** of momentum, confidence, reputation, and identity. Every time you stay quiet, play small, or "wait until things slow down," you're not just postponing your growth.

You're silently training the market to forget you exist.

It's the client who hires someone else with half your talent, but twice your visibility.

It's the podcast host who chooses your competitor, because they had a book, a framework, and a clear message you never put into words.

It's the event organizer who says, "We were looking for someone who already had a platform."

And the worst part? You see it happening all around you.

People you've mentored are now getting the recognition you crave.

Someone who just launched last year is being introduced as a "thought leader", while you're still fine-tuning your bio.

You hear someone explaining the very thing you specialize in, and it's *not even as good*, but they've got the mic. They've got the stage. They've got the authority.

It's not fair. But it's real.

Every day you stay hidden, you're leaving money, impact, and opportunities on the table. And even worse, you're starting to question your value.

This isn't just a business problem. It's a confidence problem. A slow leak in your sense of purpose. A quiet, internal erosion that says, *"Maybe I missed my window."* It's a mental tax you pay, quietly, daily, for staying small.

You start second-guessing your prices.
You shrink when you should speak up.
You spend more time trying to "prove your worth" than just owning it.

You tell yourself stories like:

- "I'm not ready."
- "I'm too busy to focus on visibility."
- "Someone else already said this."

But deep down, you know the truth:

You're not doing anything wrong.

You're just doing it in silence.

You've been showing up for everyone else. Now it's time to show up **for yourself.**

Because invisibility is not humility.
It's not strategy.
It's not sustainable.
It's suffocation.

And the longer you wait to **document, publish, and amplify your brilliance**, the more momentum you lose, and the harder it becomes to catch up. This is your line in the sand. It's time to stop being the best-kept secret. It's time to **become the obvious choice.**

Melanie's Moment: From Broadcast to Book

I'll never forget my own turning point. I had spent years in the media. I was the Vice President of a broadcasting company, running two TV stations, hosting shows, and producing hundreds of interviews. I was visible, but behind the scenes. I was helping everyone else share *their* message. But I remember the exact moment I realized I hadn't fully stepped into my own.

It was at a marketing event. A woman next to me was talking about the book she had just released. She was a coach. Less experienced than I am. But her name was all over the event signage. She was being introduced as "the author of…"

I wasn't jealous. I was awakened. It hit me like a bolt: **She had a platform. I had a resume.** So I made a decision: I would publish my first book.

Was I ready? Maybe not. Was it perfect? Definitely not. Was it powerful? Absolutely.

That one book became the foundation for everything else that followed, including speaking gigs. Strategic partnerships. Visibility on demand. And more than that, it gave me a voice. That's what I want for you.

The Inner Shift: From Expert to Authority

Before anything changes in your calendar, your client list, or your revenue, something has to change in how you *see yourself.*

This is more than a mindset. It's identity work.

The shift from **operator** to **architect** begins with a decision: "I am ready to be recognized."

This doesn't mean screaming for attention. It means stepping into your space with strategy. It means documenting your brilliance. It means giving AI, Google, and your future clients something solid to find.

This is a line-in-the-sand moment.

The Most Dangerous Beliefs We Hear (and How to Break Them)

Let's tackle the biggest excuses we hear every day, and replace them with something more powerful.

✕ "I'm not ready yet."

✓ *You're ready when you have something to say, and you already do.*

✕ "I need a bigger audience before I write a book."

✓ *A book builds your audience. Not the other way around.*

✕ "What if no one reads it?"

✓ *Someone will. And they'll become your next client, collaborator, or catalyst.*

✕ "I'm too late. The market's saturated."

✓ *There's always room for the voice that speaks with clarity, conviction, and originality.*

✕ "I'm not technical enough to use AI."

✓ *That's what we're here for. AI isn't your competition, it's your team.*

AI Doesn't Level the Playing Field.
It Exposes the Players.

There's a popular myth circulating that AI is the great equalizer. That it somehow levels the playing field for everyone. That it gives every business, coach, consultant, or creator the same shot at recognition.

Let me be clear: **that's not true.** AI doesn't reward potential. It rewards **clarity.** It amplifies what already exists.

Here's what AI will **not** do for you:

- It won't **clarify your message**. If you're still explaining what you do five different ways, AI will echo that confusion, at scale.

- It won't **give you a voice**. If you haven't defined your tone, your philosophy, your stance, AI can't reflect it.

- It won't **define your niche** or name your framework. If your business model is still abstract, generic, or jumbled, AI will churn out content that's just as forgettable.

AI is not a strategist. It's a **multiplier.** It takes what's already true about your brand and turns up the volume.

So if your ideas are scattered or invisible? Your AI assistant will publish more of that, faster. It will amplify **noise**. And worse? It'll make that noise look polished. Credible. Legitimate. And that's how your authority erodes before you even realize what's happening.

But if your book is clear. If your voice is defined. Suppose your framework is mapped, named, and published. Now AI becomes your **chief content officer**, your **top-performing sales rep**, your **brand amplifier on autopilot.**

That's when the real leverage kicks in. With the right source material, your intellectual property, your methodology, and your published message, AI can help you:

- Turn one book chapter into a dozen blog posts
- Create hundreds of social captions that sound exactly like you
- Draft emails, proposals, landing pages, and pitch decks without losing your tone
- Respond to customer inquiries and DMs in a way that builds trust, not just traffic

But AI can only multiply what you've made clear. It can't create clarity for you.

That's your job.

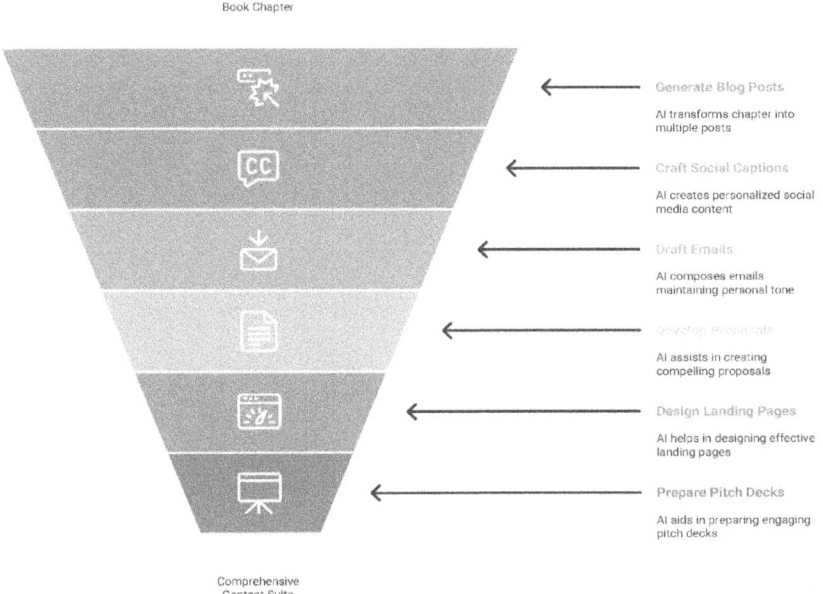

AI Content Creation Funnel

Book Chapter

Generate Blog Posts
AI transforms chapter into multiple posts

Craft Social Captions
AI creates personalized social media content

Draft Emails
AI composes emails maintaining personal tone

Develop Proposals
AI assists in creating compelling proposals

Design Landing Pages
AI helps in designing effective landing pages

Prepare Pitch Decks
AI aids in preparing engaging pitch decks

Comprehensive Content Suite

That's why **publishing your ideas**, in a book, in a manifesto, in a body of work you own, is the prerequisite.

It's your job to be the strategist. AI is the system. When your strategy is solid, when your frameworks are built, and your message is bold, AI becomes the most powerful team member you've ever had. But if you skip the foundation and hand AI your confusion, don't be surprised when it **scales your invisibility** instead of your influence.

Learning to Think AI

Let's pause for a moment and address a skill set no one taught us in school, but one that will define your visibility, scalability, and authority for years to come:

Thinking like AI.

We don't mean "thinking like a robot." We mean learning to think *with* your digital counterpart. AI isn't just a tool, it's a collaborative partner. But that partnership only works if you learn how to communicate with it. And that starts with a mindset shift:

> It's not about learning how AI thinks.
>
> It's about learning how to **organize your thinking** in a way AI can understand, scale, and share with the world.

Here's what that looks like in practice:

1. Breaking Down Your Ideas into Steps, Frameworks, and Patterns

AI thrives on clarity and structure. If your ideas live in long-winded explanations, scattered sticky notes, or spontaneous voice memos, AI can't do much with them.

But if you break your expertise into **repeatable processes, step-by-step transformations, or named frameworks**, now you've given AI a template it can multiply.

Example:

Instead of saying:

> "I help people get unstuck."

You'd say:

> "I help entrepreneurs go from idea paralysis to revenue clarity using my 3-part system: Pause, Prioritize, Publish."

Now AI can take each of those three steps and:

- Create blog posts for each stage
- Generate social content around each transformation
- Turn it into an email sequence, webinar outline, or book chapter

That's what we mean by *thinking like AI*: Make your ideas structured so that they can be scaled.

2. Asking Smart Questions

The quality of what AI gives you depends on the quality of what you ask it.

"Write me a blog post" will give you generic fluff.

But asking:

> "You are a content strategist for a financial advisor targeting six-figure millennials who want to retire early. Create five contrarian blog post titles with a bold hook and emotional resonance."

That's prompt precision.
That's AI fluency.

Learning to ask smart questions is the difference between receiving generic content and obtaining gold that resonates with you, serves your audience, and reflects your positioning.

3. Translating Your Voice into Prompts

Your voice is your brand. And AI can reflect it, if you give it the right inputs.

Here's how you do it:

- Feed AI your previous content (emails, blogs, transcripts)
- Ask it to analyze tone, rhythm, and vocabulary
- Save that voice profile as a "style guide."
- Then prompt like this:

  "Write a 500-word article on overcoming imposter syndrome. Use my brand voice: empowering, direct, warm. Start with a personal anecdote. Include one bold truth and end with a call to action."

This is how you stop sounding like a robot and start scaling your *real* voice across platforms.

4. Training AI to Write Like You, Respond Like You, Scale You

This is where the game changes.

By creating a custom GPT, or simply saving consistent prompts, you can build an AI assistant that thinks, writes, and responds like you.

Example:

Let's say you run a membership community.

You can train AI to:

- Respond to new member intros with your signature tone

- Send weekly wrap-ups that sound like your voice
- Write birthday messages, thank-yous, even proposals

When you combine this with your book and your published methodology, you now have:

- A book that proves your authority
- An AI assistant that extends it

Now your brand is working 24/7, with warmth, wisdom, and a wow factor.

This Is a New Literacy

We had to learn websites.
Then email lists.
Then social media.

Now? It's prompt engineering.
Content orchestration.
Automation logic.

The people who win next aren't just the ones who use AI.

They're the ones who **know how to think like AI and lead it.**

That means thinking in bullet points, not blobs of text. Speaking in frameworks, not free-flow. Creating assets that AI can turn into *anything*, without needing you to repeat yourself a hundred times.

And guess where this all begins?

With **publishing your thinking** in a structured, strategic form, **like a book.**

A book is your master prompt. It's your style guide. It's your AI training data.

If you want to scale your voice, codify your value, and delegate content creation without losing control, you don't need more tools. **You need a book.**

Reinvention Is Not Optional

Let's not sugarcoat this: **most people wait too long to reinvent.** They wait until the market shifts. They wait until they get burned out. They wait until someone younger, louder, or flashier starts eating their lunch.

They wait for a "wake-up call." By the time it rings, it's already too late.

> In today's world, **waiting is the most expensive strategy you can choose.**

You don't get to sit back and coast on your credentials anymore. The market doesn't care how long you've been doing it. It cares how clearly you can communicate your value **right now**, at **today's speed**, with **tomorrow's tools.**

And here's what the people who are *winning* know:

They're not just learning AI. They're **using it to design a new identity**.

They're reinventing faster than the algorithm can catch them.

- They're not service providers anymore; they're **productized brands.**
- They're not just marketers; they're **media companies.**
- They're not "just" coaches; they're **category creators.**
- They're not showing up; they're **broadcasting at scale.**
- They're not waiting for approval; they're **building their own stage.**

This isn't optional. It's essential. If you're still thinking about what to post, how to get visible, or whether now is the "right time" to write your book, **you're already behind.**

Reinvention isn't failure.
It's the **raw material of relevance.**

It's not about burning it all down. It's about burning off what no longer fits. You don't need a new logo. You need a new lens. You need a new offer, a new origin story, a new platform, and a new way of being seen.

Mike Koenigs Says It Best:

"You are either the one disrupting, or the one being disrupted."

Mike doesn't play small. He doesn't wait for permission. He moves faster than fear.

When Mike talks about reinvention, he's not talking about surface-level tweaks. He's talking about **rebuilding your business model from your identity up**, and doing it in days, not decades.

I've watched him go from video pioneer to media mogul to AI-powered digital futurist, and every time, it wasn't because the world demanded it. It was because **he chose it before it became urgent.**

That's the mindset I want you to have. Stop waiting for the pressure to build.

Apply the pressure yourself. Disrupt your own game. Change the rules while everyone else is still learning how to play.

Write the Book That Declares Your Next Chapter

You don't need to wait until you "figure it out" to write your book. You write the book to **figure it out.** You write the book that announces your evolution. You publish the version of yourself you're stepping into, before the market demands it. Because when the market looks for a leader, it finds the one who has **already claimed the idea.**

Not the one still brainstorming. Not the one still reworking their tagline. Not the one wondering if now is the time.

It's the one with the book. The framework. The category. The message.

That's the power of reinvention. That's what makes you future-proof.

So ask yourself this:

> *"If I had to start from scratch today…*
> *What version of me would I publish first?"*

If You Only Remember One Thing

> *In the age of AI, your biggest risk isn't falling behind.*
> *It's staying hidden.*

Journal Prompts: Begin the Inner Shift

Take 10 minutes and write your answers to these questions. This is the beginning of your visibility journey.

1. What message or transformation am I *already* known for, but haven't documented?
2. What am I tired of repeating over and over?
3. What future version of me do I want my book to represent?
4. What would change in my business if I were introduced as "the author of…"?
5. If I were to publish my best thinking today, what opportunities would open up tomorrow?

What's Coming: The Framework for Recognition

You don't need to do this alone.

In the pages ahead, you're going to learn how to:

- Extract your expertise
- Write your book or manifesto
- Build an AI-powered content system that scales your message
- Create frameworks that define your category
- Launch a platform that makes you the *obvious choice*

This is about building a brand that commands attention, **from people and platforms**.

Because in a world drowning in content, the only ones who rise are the ones who own their message and publish it like they mean it.

Summary: Visibility Is the New Authority

Being good at what you do is no longer enough. In a digital world driven by AI, search engines, and algorithms, the experts who rise to the top are not the most qualified; they're the most *visible* and *positioned*. This chapter introduced the central idea of the book: **Visibility is the new authority.** You must publish your message, claim your space, and train the world (and the machines) to recognize your voice.

A book is not a vanity project. It's the flagship asset of your Authority Platform. It gives your message structure, power, and permanence. And when paired with AI, it becomes a visibility engine that works for you 24/7.

Action Items

1. **Install the new mindset.**

   Write down: *I am no longer waiting to be discovered. I am publishing to be recognized.*

2. **Commit to your book.**

   Block 30 minutes this week to brainstorm your core message. This is the seed of your book.

3. **Audit your visibility.**

   Google yourself. Ask: "Does what's visible match what I want to be known for?"

4. **Write your first book prompt.**

   Open ChatGPT. Prompt: "Help me outline a book based on my process for helping [ideal client] achieve [transformation]."

5. **Name the cost of staying invisible.**

   What has it already cost you in missed opportunities, undercharging, or burnout?

6. **Share your first piece of thought leadership.**

   Pull a line from your book draft or framework and post it. Start the echo.

CHAPTER 2

THE FIVE PILLARS OF
AI BUSINESS TRANSFORMATION

The measure of intelligence is the ability to change.

–Albert Einstein

When I start working with someone new, I don't just start throwing a bunch of tools at them. That's like handing someone a toolkit and expecting them to build a house without a blueprint. Instead, I provide them with a clear path, which I call the Five Pillars of AI Business Transformation. It helps take all the guesswork out of it and makes it practical. We get focused on where AI can actually reduce friction, create leverage, and give us back what we all need more of: time.

And let me tell you, I don't just talk about AI because it's trendy. I use it every single day in our business to buy back time and scale the things that really matter. One of the biggest game changers for us was utilizing AI for podcast clipping, blog drafting, and content repurposing. What used to take my team 12 to 15 hours a week? Now we're doing it in under 2. That's not theory. That's the time we now get to spend on strategy, client work, and the things that actually move the needle.

AI isn't some far-off thing. It's here, and it's changing everything: how we work, how we compete, how we grow. For me, integrating AI hasn't been about chasing the latest thing. It's been about building more intelligent systems that let us spend our time where it counts: being creative, being strategic, and being leaders.

The Five Pillars of AI Business Transformation

The Five Pillars of AI Business Transformation didn't just pop out of thin air one afternoon while we were sipping coffee. Nope! They came straight from the brainpower of a fantastic AI mastermind Team led by Mike Koenigs, Brad Costanzo, and Joe Fier. Powerhouse guys who are trailblazing the innovative use of AI in business. They didn't just show us tools; they gave us a whole new way to think. A new way to build your business to be faster, smarter, and yes, even more human. We rolled up our sleeves, tested everything they taught us, and now we are giving it to you, step by step, because it's too good not to share.

Here it is the **Five Pillars of AI Business Transformation.**

- **Brainstorming:** This is all about idea generation. AI is phenomenal for unlocking creativity and breaking through mental blocks. Need content ideas? New angles for your book or offer? This is where we start.

- **Building:** Think creation and implementation. We use AI to help draft content, structure frameworks, build pages, and more. It helps get version one out the door faster than ever.

- **Connecting:** This is about outreach and engagement. AI helps us write emails, build outreach campaigns, and connect with new audiences, without it taking all day.

- **Investigating:** Use AI to research, analyze data, and synthesize information. From competitive analysis to trend spotting, this pillar keeps you sharp and informed.

- **Streamlining:** My favorite. Automating repetitive tasks and simplifying processes so you can do more with less. From client onboarding to content scheduling, this is where you reclaim your time.

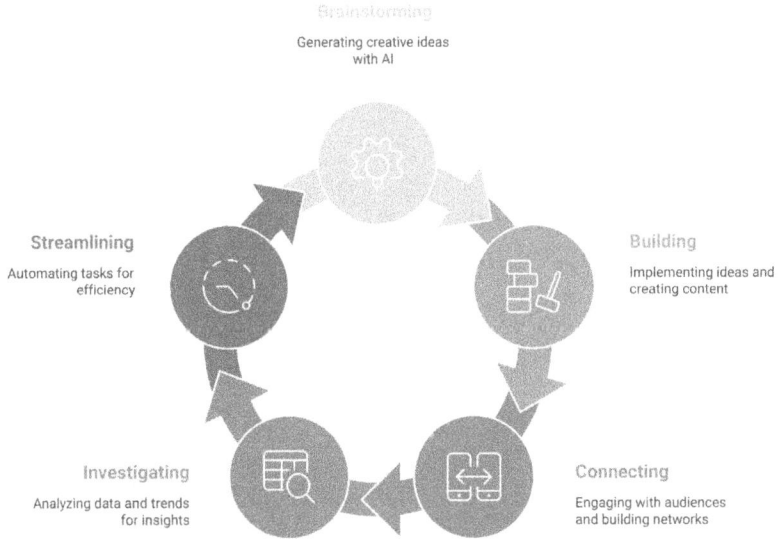

AI-Driven Productivity Cycle

Brainstorming
Generating creative ideas with AI

Streamlining
Automating tasks for efficiency

Building
Implementing ideas and creating content

Investigating
Analyzing data and trends for insights

Connecting
Engaging with audiences and building networks

These five pillars are how we've made AI work across every part of our business. They help us think bigger, move faster, and get more done without burning out.

This isn't about plugging in a tool and hoping it works. It's about embedding intelligence into your daily workflow, shifting how your team thinks, and building a business that's agile, adaptive, and future-ready.

Because here's what I know: the businesses that embrace AI as a strategic partner are going to lead the next decade. And I want that for you.

Pillar 1: Brainstorming – AI as a Cognitive Amplifier

AI isn't just a tool, it's your new power partner. Think of it like having a virtual board member or strategic advisor who's available 24/7. I use AI every day to brainstorm, map out content, test new business models, and uncover opportunities that most people miss. It helps me make faster, smarter decisions, whether I'm planning a launch, building a brand, or scaling a company. It's like having a supercharged business coach in your back pocket, ready to spark ideas, analyze trends, and guide your next big move.

This is where the magic starts. When I talk about brainstorming, I mean truly immersing oneself in the creative process. Whether you're dreaming up a new offer, plotting a launch, or solving a thorny client challenge, this is where AI becomes your ultimate thinking partner.

Imagine having a brainstorming partner that's always on, always ready to help you cook up your next big idea. I treat AI like a virtual board member who's sitting right there with me at the whiteboard. I'll ask, "Hey, help me create a marketing plan for Gen X homeowners." And just like that, I've got a starting point, and usually more ideas than I bargained for!

Brainstorming is the foundation of every creative and strategic move we make. And here's the secret: AI supercharges it. It can scan massive datasets, spot patterns you might miss, and provide a new lens through which to view your problem.

And it's not just about throwing a hundred ideas at the wall. AI helps shape those ideas. It clusters similar ones, summarizes key points, adjusts the tone, and makes everything clearer. It keeps things moving when your brain wants to hit pause.

Think about it like this: if you're working with a sustainable pet food brand trying to win over millennial dog parents, the ones who feed their pups organic kale and bone broth smoothies, and you hit a creative wall, you can turn to AI. You ask, "What are 10 unique value propositions for this kind of brand?" And boom! It might throw out things like "farm-to-bowl freshness" or "gut-health formulas for happier pets." That kind of brainstorming input is priceless.

But here's the thing, AI will only be as good as the prompts you give it. You have to know what to ask. And once you do, it's like turning on a faucet of creativity that doesn't shut off.

So remember this: AI won't replace your creativity. It enhances it. It gives you momentum when you're stuck and turns your sparks into strategies. And when you combine that with clear positioning and a strong brand message? That's when you become unstoppable.

Pillar 2: Building – Laying the Bricks with AI

Let's talk about building. You've got your ideas from brainstorming, now it's time to bring them to life. AI can be a helpful tool here.

Think of it like a digital assistant that helps you move faster. You can use AI to draft blog posts, outline emails, sketch out social media content, or even generate visuals. It helps you get started, and often it can make the whole process feel a lot less overwhelming.

For example, if you need a slideshow for a presentation, a tool like Gamma AI can build one in seconds. If you're looking to put together a short video, something like InVideo can help shape your message into a simple, polished clip. Tools like Oasis AI can turn a single idea into different types of content, from tweets to full articles.

Here's an example story. Sarah, who leads marketing at a financial firm, needed to create five different guides for five different types of clients. Each one had to have its own message, look, and style. Usually, that kind of project would take a few weeks and require a whole team.

Instead, Sarah used Claude to draft the content. She tried Sora to generate illustrations. Then Descript to add voiceovers for videos. What should have taken a month only took a few days. Her team spent their time reviewing and adjusting instead of starting from scratch.

That's the benefit. AI didn't do everything. It just got them past the blank page faster.

If you're using AI to build, keep it simple. Start with the tools that fit what you need. Let them help you draft and design, but always make time to review, refine, and make it yours.

This is not about getting everything perfect on the first try. It's about having a starting point that helps you move forward without feeling stuck.

Pillar 3: Connecting – Weaving AI Into the Heart of Your Business

AI is transforming how we connect with leads, clients, and even our teams. From smart chatbots to personalized messaging and voice assistants, it's all about creating faster, more meaningful interactions. You're not just automating replies, you're delivering 24/7 responsiveness with a personal touch that makes people feel seen, heard, and valued.

Alright, let's talk about connecting the dots, because when it comes to AI, it's not just about having the tech. It's about pulling everything together: your people, your systems, your data, your workflows. This pillar is all about breaking down silos and building a 360-degree view, so your business runs smarter, faster, and more connected than ever before.

So here's the thing. You can't just drop AI into one department and hope for magic. That's like planting a seed in a closet and expecting sunshine to appear. Leaders need visibility across the entire organization, enabling them to see how everything links together, so they can make decisions that are not only confident but also strategically aligned with where the business is headed.

Let's start with mapping the whole picture. You have to know how everything fits together, including processes, platforms, and teams. When you zoom out and see the entire landscape, those hidden opportunities and risks become visible. You catch things you'd never notice if you're only looking at one piece of the puzzle.

Now let's talk about your people. We've seen it time and time again: if you want successful AI adoption, you must bring your team along. That means showing them the possibilities, giving them the tools, and creating those "aha" moments through real-time guidance and practical training. And leaders? You've got to lead by example. When people see you embracing new ways of thinking, it builds trust. And don't forget those natural influencers in your company, get them involved early. They're the ones who'll spark enthusiasm and help the change really take root.

Another big one, trust. You've got to be transparent about how and where AI is being used. That means clear governance, strong data privacy policies, and regular check-ins to keep everything on track. Trust is the bridge between innovation and adoption.

And finally, keep the momentum going. Transformation isn't a one-and-done project. It's a living, breathing process. AI can actually help here too, flagging issues before they escalate and pointing out new opportunities as they come up. That's how you stay agile and ahead of the game.

Now here's something I want you to remember: you can build the most sophisticated AI system in the world, but if your people aren't on board, if they don't feel connected to it, it won't fly. Building and connecting go hand-in-hand. Every piece of feedback, every bump in the road, all feed back into making your AI systems better, stronger, and more aligned with your culture.

Staying connected with your audience is crucial, and AI can help you do it more effectively. Think email automation, chatbots that answer customer questions around the clock, and personalized messages that resonate. We even created an ROI bot for our website! I'm not the most technical person, but even I could see the power in that.

Communication is no longer a one-size-fits-all proposition. With AI, every message can be tailored to the individual recipient based on their behavior, preferences, and history with your brand. This level of personalization was once reserved for enterprise businesses with massive marketing departments; now it's available to solo entrepreneurs and small teams.

In today's world, fast and personal communication isn't just a "nice to have," it's a *must* if you want to stay ahead of the competition. Take Michael, for example. He runs this charming boutique travel agency that creates custom European vacations. But his small team was completely swamped. Client inquiries would flood in, especially at night when everyone had logged off for the day. And with customers sometimes waiting 12 hours or more for a simple answer, he was losing bookings left and right to those big guys with 24/7 call centers.

Michael knew he needed a solution, and fast. So he brought in an AI-powered chatbot for his website. And let me tell you, the transformation was like flipping a switch. Overnight, the chatbot started handling about 78% of the first client's questions all by itself, giving instant answers about destination ideas, visa info, and package pricing, all with incredible accuracy.

For example, there was this one family planning their dream trip to Italy. The chatbot spent 15 minutes chatting with them, at 11 o'clock at night, gathering all their must-haves, budget details, and sightseeing dreams. By the time Michael's team got into the office the next morning, they didn't have to start from scratch. They had a full profile in hand and could immediately jump into crafting a gorgeous, personalized itinerary.

What surprised me most was that the chatbot didn't make the service feel more robotic; it actually made the relationships with the clients *better*. People felt cared for right away, and by the time the team followed up, they could focus on the exciting stuff, the high-value conversations, instead of collecting basic information.

The results? Bookings shot up, their conversion rate jumped by 34% in just the first quarter, and their client reviews kept raving about how *responsive* and *attentive* they were. And the best part? Michael didn't have to hire a single new employee.

Now that's what I call smart communication, and smart business.

Pillar 4: Investigating – Unlocking Deeper Insight and Smarter Risk Management with AI

AI lets you cut through the noise and get straight to what matters. It spots patterns, predicts trends, and hands you insights you can actually use. I rely on it to make faster, sharper decisions, because in business, clarity and timing are everything.

Let's dig into something powerful: how AI is completely reshaping how we uncover insights and manage risk. I call this pillar "Investigating," and it's like putting a magnifying glass on your business with a little extra brainpower behind it. It's not just about organizing data or finding answers faster; it's about changing the way you think, the way you make decisions, and how quickly you can act on what you discover.

Now, here's the exciting part. Imagine asking a question, just like you would in a conversation, and having an AI tool sift through mountains of documents to find the exact answer, with sources to back it up. No more endless scrolling or guessing at search terms. These tools do it in real time, helping your team pivot and adapt as new information comes in. It's efficient, it's smart, and it saves time, tons of it.

We also see AI powering predictive analytics. Think of it as your future radar. Whether it's spotting equipment issues before they happen or understanding what your customer wants before they even ask, AI is giving businesses a whole new level of insight. You're not just reacting anymore, you're getting ahead of the game.

And when it comes to big decisions, AI's right there with you. It's uncovering trends and patterns in the data that would take a team of people weeks to figure out. It's your silent partner in the room, offering insight that's backed by millions of data points.

This gets even more meaningful in high-stakes areas, such as fraud, cyber threats, and intellectual property issues. AI helps investigators spot the subtle stuff, the things that might slip past the human eye. That's what makes it such a strong asset for risk management.

And get this, AI doesn't just support the investigation; it actually helps prep for interviews too. It can suggest questions, simulate responses, and organize information so you walk in ready. Same with writing reports. AI takes your notes, codes, and documents and creates a summary of summaries, clean, organized, and presentation-ready.

But let's not forget how we use AI, matters. You've got to have responsible data practices in place. That means being transparent about where your data comes from, checking for bias, tracking changes, and making sure your AI stays fair and compliant. Assigning ownership within your team is key; someone has to be accountable for keeping everything above board.

Data is the lifeblood of informed decisions, but who has the time to wade through mountains of it? AI can analyze your marketing campaigns, customer feedback, and even compare contracts to tell you what's changed! I remember when someone sent us an updated contract. Instead of spending hours reading the fine print, I just had AI tell me the key differences and suggest how to respond. Talk about a time saver!

The analysis capabilities of AI extend far beyond basic metrics. Today's tools can identify subtle patterns in customer behavior, predict market trends before they're obvious to everyone else, and give you insights that would have required a team of data scientists just a few years ago.

When you leverage AI for analysis, you're essentially gaining a superpower, the ability to see connections and opportunities invisible to competitors still relying on traditional methods.

Sometimes the answers you need are hiding in plain sight, and it takes the right tools to uncover them.

Take Rachel, for example. She's the founder of a specialty coffee subscription service, you know, the kind that delivers amazing, handpicked beans right to your doorstep. Business seemed great, reviews were fantastic, but Rachel noticed something unsettling: customers weren't sticking around as long as they used to. Her team had collected mountains of data, purchase histories, survey responses, and feedback forms, but they just couldn't connect the dots.

That's when Rachel decided it was time to dig deeper. She brought in an AI analytics tool, and let me tell you, it was a game-changer. The AI scanned thousands of customer interactions and spotted a pattern that the team had completely missed. Subscribers who received specific coffee bean varieties in their first two shipments were more likely to stay loyal. Even more surprising, the AI picked up subtle language patterns hinting that brewing difficulty was a major frustration for customers who eventually canceled, even though they never said it outright. The real magic? It wasn't just *what* was happening; it was understanding *why* it was happening.

Here's the real takeaway: analyzing your data the right way doesn't just tell you what's going wrong, it shows you how to make it right. And when you have that kind of deep understanding, you can transform your entire business.

Pillar 5: Streamlining – Making Business Smoother, Smarter, and More Scalable with AI

This is where AI becomes a force multiplier. I use it to take repetitive tasks off my plate, follow-ups, scheduling, and even parts of the sales process. It's not just automation for the sake of convenience; it's about running a tighter, more efficient business so I can stay focused on vision and growth.

We all love making life easier, and our business runs better. That's what this "Streamlining" pillar is all about. With AI in your corner, you're not just working harder, you're working smarter. It's about turning the tedious into automatic, the complicated into simple, and the slow into lightning-fast.

So, what does that look like in real-time?

First up, *Automating the Routine.* Think of AI as that dependable team member who never sleeps, doesn't need coffee breaks, and gets things done right every time. Whether it's handling emails, sorting invoices, scheduling appointments, or answering customer questions through a chatbot, AI clears the clutter. That frees up your team to focus on the big stuff: strategy, creativity, and innovation.

Then there's *boosting operations across the board.* From manufacturing and logistics to retail and finance, AI is helping businesses predict problems before they happen, manage inventory in real time, and make smarter decisions faster. It's not just about cutting costs; it's about delivering better service, faster turnaround, and a smoother experience for everyone involved, especially your customers.

And let's not forget *user experience*. AI tools today are sharp; they know how to personalize the journey for both your clients and your employees. Everything becomes more intuitive, more responsive, and just easier. AI helps remove the guesswork. It serves up exactly what you need, when you need it. That's a game-changer for engagement and productivity.

But here's the part I really love: *creating new opportunities*. AI levels the playing field. Smaller companies can now do what only big enterprises used to pull off. You've got a tiny team? AI can help you launch campaigns, enter new markets, or build tools that would've cost a fortune five years ago. Whether you're a boutique firm or a solo entrepreneur, AI helps you move like a giant, without losing your agility.

Now, here's something deeper to think about. Streamlining your internal operations isn't just about doing things better inside your business. It positions you to do more outside your business. The faster and smarter you operate internally, the more attractive you become to partners, suppliers, and even customers. AI makes your business more flexible, more collaborative, and more valuable in the broader ecosystem.

So yeah, "streamlining" might sound like tightening the ship, but really, it's expanding your reach, your impact, and your opportunities.

This is where you can really see immediate results. Think about all those repetitive tasks that eat up your valuable time; AI can streamline them. Automating lead generation from Zoom meetings, setting up automated email sequences, these are things that can free you up to focus on the bigger picture. I even figured out how to take screenshots of attendees in a Zoom mastermind I was part of, upload them to AI, and generate a spreadsheet of everyone's names, allowing me to connect with them on LinkedIn and automate those connection requests.

Automation isn't just about efficiency; it's about creating systems that work while you sleep. The most successful entrepreneurs aren't working 80-hour weeks; they're building automated systems that multiply their impact without multiplying their time investment.

Let me tell you a quick story that I just love because it's the perfect reminder of why you can't afford to be complacent, especially in today's world where change is moving at lightning speed!

Remember Blockbuster? Oh my gosh, Blockbuster was *the place* to be on a Friday night. You'd walk in, grab your popcorn, pick out a couple of movies, and just have the best weekend. They thought they were good enough. They thought, "Hey, everyone loves coming to the store, grabbing videos. We're golden!"

But guess what? Netflix had a new idea. They saw the future, streaming movies from the comfort of your couch! They actually went to Blockbuster and said, "Hey, why don't we team up? We could do something really special together." And you know what Blockbuster said? They laughed them out of the room. Yep. Turned them down flat.

And we all know how that story ended, right? Netflix became a giant—a household name. Blockbuster? Well, the only place you can find Blockbuster these days is in a meme or a museum.

Here's the thing: it's easy to get comfortable. It's easy to say, "What I'm doing is good enough." But good enough is not *good enough* anymore. If you're not evolving, you're dissolving. Period.

So what's the lesson here? You've got to see the wave before it hits you. You have to innovate, take action, and be willing to change. And guess what? Building your personal brand, writing your book, telling your story, that's part of catching the wave. That's part of making sure *you* don't become the next Blockbuster.

I don't know about you, but I want to be the Netflix of my industry. Always thinking ahead, always reaching new people, always growing. And I want that for you too! So don't wait. Your future is too important.

Just like the lumberjack had to learn to use the chainsaw to stay competitive, we need to learn to wield the power of AI. It's not about being replaced; it's about being supercharged.

Summary

AI can transform your business when you understand the **Five Key Pillars of AI Business Transformation: Brainstorming, Building, Connecting, Investigating, and Streamlining**. It acts as your brainstorming partner, speeds up content creation, personalizes customer communication, uncovers powerful insights from data, and eliminates time-wasting tasks. By focusing on these five areas, you can move faster, serve better, and build a business that scales without exhausting you.

Action Items

1. Use AI to **brainstorm** ideas or solve a business problem.
2. **Build** or create one piece of content (post, article, graphic) using an AI tool.
3. Set up an AI tool to automate a customer communication task to **connect** with your audience.
4. **Investigate** one set of business data with AI to find new insights.
5. **Streamline** one repetitive task to save time and increase efficiency.

The Five Key Pillars of AI Business Transformation: Core Definitions and Strategic Focus

Pillar Name	Core Definition	Strategic Focus
Brainstorming	Leveraging AI-powered tools to generate, expand, organize, and refine ideas, augmenting human creativity and problem-solving.	Accelerating innovation, overcoming creative blocks, and structuring nascent ideas for strategic development.
Building	Establishing the foundational elements, strategic vision, robust data infrastructure, scalable technology, and organizational capabilities for successful AI adoption.	Creating a resilient and adaptable base for long-term AI-driven growth and operational excellence.
Connecting	Fostering seamless integration and collaboration across systems, data, workflows, and people to achieve holistic organizational visibility and AI adoption.	Ensuring AI initiatives are integrated, trusted, and supported by a unified, empowered workforce.

Investigating	Utilizing AI's analytical power to uncover deep insights from vast datasets, predict outcomes, and manage risks, enhancing decision-making and compliance.	Driving data-driven intelligence, mitigating threats, and enabling proactive strategic responses.
Streamlining	Optimizing operational workflows and business processes through AI-driven automation, efficiency gains, and enhanced user experiences.	Reducing costs, increasing productivity, improving service delivery, and unlocking new business opportunities.

AI's Transformative Impact Across the Pillars: Key Benefits and Illustrative Examples

Pillar Name	Key Benefits	Illustrative Examples
Brainstorming	Accelerates idea generation and exploration. Overcomes creative blocks and provides structure. Augments human creativity for deeper insights.	AI generates 20+ blog post ideas in seconds for a marketing team. An AI chatbot helps a product development team explore alternative design framings for a new app.
Building	Establishes a robust foundation for AI scalability. Ensures data quality and governance for reliable AI. Aligns AI initiatives with strategic business goals.	A financial firm centralizes disparate customer data into a data lake for AI model training. An organization invests in reskilling programs for employees to manage new AI tools and processes.

Connecting	Fosters holistic organizational visibility. Enhances cross-functional collaboration and communication. Drives widespread AI adoption through trust and empowerment.	AI maps interconnected IT systems and workflows to identify hidden dependencies before a major system upgrade. Personalized AI training paths are delivered to employees based on their learning styles and tech-savviness.
Investigating	Uncovers deep insights from vast, complex datasets. Enhances risk management and fraud detection. Streamlines complex investigations and report generation.	GenAI sifts through petabytes of legal documents to identify key evidence in a fraud investigation. An AI system predicts equipment failures in a manufacturing plant based on sensor data, preventing costly downtime.
Streamlining	Automates routine tasks, freeing human capital. Boosts operational efficiency and cost control. Improves user experience and creates new business models.	AI-powered chatbots handle 80% of basic customer service inquiries 24/7. A retail company uses AI for smart inventory management, optimizing stock levels, and reducing waste.

CHAPTER 3

FROM DABBLER TO DOMINATOR: POSITIONING YOURSELF AS A CATEGORY KING

In order to be irreplaceable, one must always be different.

–Coco Chanel

There's a silent war being waged every single day in the marketplace. It isn't fought with armies or weapons, but with ideas, content, and the relentless hum of the digital world. It is the war for attention, for relevance, and ultimately, for authority. In this war, simply being good at what you do is no longer a viable strategy. Competence has become a commodity. Being an "expert" is the new table stakes. If you want not just to survive but thrive, you must stop trying to be the best and start striving to be the only.

When I work with clients, I see a clear and predictable pattern in how entrepreneurs approach the monumental shift that is Artificial Intelligence. It's a journey with three distinct stages, and where you are on this path will determine the entire trajectory of your business for the next decade.

First, there are the "Deniers." This might remind you of my own mom, a wonderful woman who, back in the late 90s, was thoroughly convinced that the internet was just a passing fad for computer geeks. The Deniers today see AI as either a novelty, a threat to their established ways, or something too complex to bother with. They are clinging to the "old way" of doing things, believing their established skills and hard work will be enough to carry them through. They are betting against a tidal wave, and history has never been kind to those who make that bet. Hopefully, if you're reading this book, you are not a Denier.

Next, and this is where the vast majority of well-intentioned experts reside, are the "Dabblers." The Dabblers are curious and smart. They've opened up ChatGPT. They've asked them to write a poem or maybe draft a clever email. They've seen a flicker of the magic. I even coached a brilliant college student recently, a digital native you'd think would be all-in, who told me she'd only been on ChatGPT a handful of times. And I had this overwhelming urge to say, "Oh my gosh, you have to dive deeper! You're standing at the edge of the ocean and only dipping your toes in!"

The Dabbler's experience is one of inconsistent, often frustrating, novelty. They use AI like a slightly more advanced search engine, not as a strategic partner. They lack a system, a framework for turning their raw power into tangible business results. They feel a bit like they're missing out, but they haven't yet had the "aha" moment that transforms their entire approach.

And then, there are the "Dominators." This is where the magic happens. This is where I encourage, plead, and push every single one of you to be. The Dominator doesn't just use AI; they think with AI. They see it not as a tool to do old things faster, but as a partner to architect entirely new ways of creating value, building authority, and owning their market. They are not fighting the future; they are co-creating it. The sooner you embrace the mindset and the systems of the Dominator, the further and faster ahead you are going to be, creating an ever-widening gap between you and everyone else still stuck in the Dabbler stage.

Why a Book Is Your First Dominator Move

The minute you write and publish a business book, one that articulates your point of view, outlines your signature framework, and plants a flag around your unique philosophy, you do something most experts never do:

You stop being interchangeable.

A book is not just a collection of your ideas; it's the anchor of your personal monopoly. It's how you carve your category into stone and say to the world, "This is what I believe. This is what I solve. And this is how I'm different."

When you become a published author with a defined framework and a clear market niche, everything else accelerates:

- Your content strategy becomes easier to scale
- Your offers become clearer and higher-ticket
- Your inbound leads become more qualified
- Your visibility is algorithmically favored (AI loves authority assets)
- And most importantly, your confidence expands, because your ideas finally live somewhere permanent

Before you can dominate a market, you must first declare what space is yours. A book is that declaration. It is your blueprint. Your billboard. Your positioning, made tangible.

This chapter is your roadmap to making that leap. But it begins with a truth that AI, for all its power, cannot solve on its own: If you don't have a clear, powerful, and unique position in the market, AI will just help you become a more efficient nobody.

The Great Commodity Trap: Why Most Experts Stay Invisible

Let's diagnose the single biggest reason why talented, hardworking experts fail to gain traction. Most of them describe what they do with a simple, logical, and utterly forgettable formula: "I help [X] do [Y] with [Z]."

- "I help small business owners increase their revenue with digital marketing."
- "I help executives become better leaders with one-on-one coaching."
- "I help SaaS companies generate more leads with content marketing."

Listen closely. Can you hear the sound of a thousand other consultants, coaches, and agencies saying the exact same thing? When your message is interchangeable, your business becomes interchangeable. You are dropped into a vast, crowded, and brutal "Red Ocean" teeming with sharks, all fighting over the same small pool of clients.

In this environment, you are forced to compete on the only metrics left: price and effort. You have to hustle harder, make more calls, write more proposals, and inevitably, lower your prices to win a deal. You could be ten times more skilled, more dedicated, and more effective than your competition, but if you're positioned inside a crowded category, the market will treat you as just another commodity. And the market has no loyalty to commodities; it only cares about the lowest price.

This is the great commodity trap, and it is a soul-crushing race to the bottom. The antidote is not to become better, but to become different.

The solution is to stop competing and start creating. You must move from being in the market to being the market. You must become a Category King.

What is a Category King? (And Why It's the Only Goal That Matters)

A Category King isn't just a market leader. A market leader fights for the biggest slice of an existing pie. A Category King bakes a whole new pie, and for a long time, they are the only ones selling it. They fundamentally redefine a problem and, in doing so, create and own an entirely new category in the minds of their customers.

Think about it:

Apple did not invent the MP3 player. There were dozens of clunky, complicated devices on the market. Apple created the category of the "iPod," which stood for "1,000 songs in your pocket." They didn't sell a device; they sold effortless access to your entire music library. They defined the game, and everyone else was forced to play by their rules.

Salesforce did not invent Customer Relationship Management (CRM) software. It was a billion-dollar industry dominated by clunky, server-based systems from giants like Siebel. Marc Benioff created the category of cloud-based SaaS with the mantra of "No Software." He didn't sell a better CRM; he sold a new, simpler, and more accessible way of doing business.

Dave Ramsey did not invent financial advice. The world was full of financial planners talking about mutual funds and asset allocation. Dave Ramsey created the category of "debt-free living" for middle-class America. He created a new language ("baby steps," "gazelle intensity") and a simple, powerful philosophy. He doesn't compete with other financial advisors; he operates in a universe of his own creation.

These Dominators didn't just offer a product or service; they offered a new perspective. They created a new language. They established a new "Point of View" that changed how people thought about a problem or an opportunity. Category Kings don't chase clients because their category acts as a gravitational force, pulling the right people toward them. They aren't just an option in the market; they are the starting point of the conversation.

If you truly want to leverage AI to build an unassailable brand, you don't just need content. You need a category.

Your Blueprint for Category Creation: The Three Foundations

So, how do you do it? How do you carve out your own kingdom in a world full of noise? It's a three-step process of strategic carving, not competitive fighting.

Foundation 1: Choose a Hyper-Specific Niche (Your Plot of Land)

The biggest fear most entrepreneurs have is "niching down." They believe that by narrowing their focus, they are shrinking their opportunities. The opposite is true. In the age of the internet, specificity is the key to scalability. A broad, generic message whispers to everyone and resonates with no one. A sharp, specific message shouts to a select few, and they hear it loud and clear.

Your niche is the plot of land where you will build your kingdom. It must be specific enough that you can become the undisputed #1 expert within it.

Look at these transformations:

- From "business coach" to "leadership coach for first-time, VC-backed SaaS founders navigating their Series A funding round."

- From "real estate investor" to "multifamily syndicator specializing in converting B-class properties into tech-enabled communities for traveling nurses."
- From "health coach" to "a guide helping post-menopausal women reclaim their energy and metabolic health through ketogenic cycling."

Can you feel the difference? The generic expert has to explain their value from scratch every single time. The specific expert's value is self-evident to their target audience. The moment a first-time SaaS founder hears that description, a light goes on in their head: "That's me. That person gets my exact problem."

Action: Niche Clarity

Take out a piece of paper right now. Write down your current, generic description. Now, answer these three questions to add layers of specificity:

1. Who is the most specific audience I can serve? (Think industry, job title, stage of business, a specific psychographic profile.)
2. What is the most painful and expensive problem this specific audience has that I am uniquely equipped to solve?
3. What is the unique context surrounding their problem? (E.g., market shifts, technological changes, a specific life stage.)

Don't be afraid to go "too narrow." You can always expand later, but you must first establish a beachhead of authority in a well-defined niche.

Foundation 2: Attach Your Name to a Big Idea (Plant Your Flag)

Your niche is the "who." Your Big Idea is the "what." This is your unique philosophy, your contrarian viewpoint, your named solution that becomes synonymous with your brand. This is the flag you plant on your plot of land.

This is where you stop talking about the "service" you provide (coaching, marketing, consulting) and start talking about the idea you represent.

Examples from our own world:

- We don't just sell "AI consulting." We champion the "AI Authority Engine."

- We don't just offer "book coaching." We guide people through "High-Ticket Reinvention with AI Publishing."

- Our target market isn't just "experts." We are calling out to "AI for Thought Leaders."

Your Big Idea gives people a handle to grasp. It's memorable. It's ownable. It separates you from everyone else who is still just selling a generic service. What is the one core concept, the one unique lens through which you see the world, that you can put a name to? It could be a powerful metaphor, a contrarian take, or a new way of framing an old problem. Brainstorm it, name it, and then start using that language relentlessly.

Foundation 3: Create and Name Your Signature IP (Build Your Fortress)

If your Big Idea is the "what," your Signature IP is the "how." This is your proprietary framework, your step-by-step system, your unique methodology that makes your thinking tangible and transferable. It's the proof that you don't just have a clever idea; you have a proven process for delivering results.

This is arguably the most powerful asset you can create. When you give your frameworks names, people can remember them, repeat them, and most importantly, pay you for them. It transforms you from a service provider who trades time for money into an intellectual property owner who licenses their unique system.

Our "AI Authority Engine" is not just a clever name; it's a fortress built on four distinct pillars that we can teach, implement, and scale:

1. Book-as-a-Brand: Using a book as the cornerstone of authority.
2. The Content Flywheel: A system for turning one core idea into hundreds of content assets.
3. Category King Positioning: The very strategy you are learning right now.
4. Scalable Monetization: Moving from one-to-one services to one-to-many offers.

By naming and defining this process, we've created something tangible. A client isn't just hiring us; they are investing in implementing the "AI Authority Engine" in their business. It feels more real, more structured, and infinitely more valuable than just "hiring a consultant."

Action: Frame Your Genius

What is your process? Map out the 3 to 7 key steps you take a client through to get them from their "before" state to their "after" state. Now, give that process a compelling, memorable name. This is your V1 Signature IP. Sketch it out. Make it visual. This is the blueprint for your fortress.

AI: The Great Multiplier of Category Power

Let's return to our central theme. If you are a commodity with AI, you are just a faster, more efficient commodity. You're a nobody with a megaphone, shouting generic messages into the void more quickly.

But if you have followed these steps, if you have carved a clear niche, planted a flag with a Big Idea, and built a fortress of Signature IP, then AI becomes the most powerful force multiplier in history. It takes your unique, well-defined category and amplifies it at an exponential scale.

With a clear category, you can now use AI as your tireless Chief Content Officer to:

- Write Your Category-Defining Book: Feed your Signature IP, case studies, and niche research into an AI and have it help you draft a 50,000-word book that establishes you as the undisputed thought leader in your category.

- Generate an Army of Content Assets: Turn every chapter of your book into a signature talk, a webinar, a lead magnet, and a series of 100+ social media posts, all reinforcing your unique category and frameworks.

- Build Your Authority Funnel: Use AI to write the copy for your landing pages, your email sequences, your video scripts, and your workshop outlines, all designed to attract your ideal niche client and indoctrinate them into your Big Idea.

- Dominate Search and Social: Leverage AI to identify the exact questions your niche audience is asking online, and then create perfectly optimized content that makes you the first and only answer they find.

Building Authority with AI

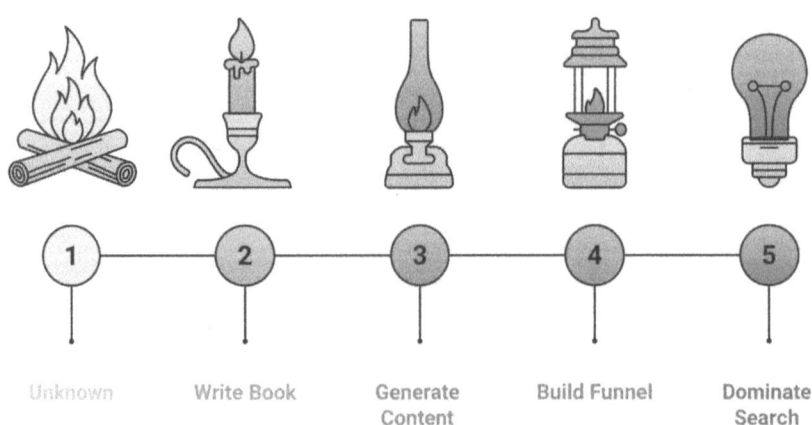

| Unknown | Write Book | Generate Content | Build Funnel | Dominate Search |

AI doesn't create your category, but it builds your kingdom on top of it with breathtaking speed and efficiency.

The One-Sentence Power Positioning Formula: Your Million-Dollar Mantra

Now let's distill all of this strategic work into a single, powerful sentence that you can use on your website, in your bio, and at the start of every sales conversation. When nailed, this formula is worth millions in clarity and client attraction.

"I help [WHO - Your Niche] achieve [TRANSFORMATION] using my [UNIQUE METHOD - Your Signature IP/Category]."

Notice how this elevates the generic "I help X do Y" formula into something with power, specificity, and intrigue.

Let's look at some examples:

- Generic: "I help coaches get more clients."

- Power Positioning: "I help 7-figure coaches escape the 'time for money' trap and build a scalable group program using my 5-Pillar Freedom Framework."

- Generic: "I'm a fractional CMO for tech companies."

- Power Positioning: "I help fractional CMOs dominate their industry by building personal category empires through my AI Publishing Accelerator."

Plug yours in now. Seriously, stop reading and write it down. This sentence is your battle cry. It's the ultimate litmus test for the clarity of your positioning. If you can't state it simply, you haven't done the strategic work.

A Story of Reinvention: How We Became Our Own Case Study

I don't want this to feel like abstract theory. I want to share a little behind-the-scenes story of how we, at Elite Online Publishing, didn't just talk about adapting to AI, but rolled up our sleeves and used these exact principles to reinvent our own company.

For years, we were a successful book publishing company. But we saw the writing on the wall. The world was moving too fast. Just being a publisher wasn't going to be enough. We were in danger of becoming a commodity. We knew we had to make a "Dominator" move.

So we made a wild decision: we were going to create and launch an entirely new offer, a new category for ourselves, not over months or weeks, but in a single, hyper-focused weekend.

We locked ourselves in a room. We used our own frameworks. We defined our new category: not just "publishing," but the "AI Authority Engine." We then used AI as our strategic partner.

Over the course of about 48 hours, we:

- Outlined and wrote an Entire Book to launch the new category (in fact, you are reading the result of that weekend sprint right now).

- Built a Brand-New Landing Page with compelling copy that spoke directly to our new niche. Go to BeRecongnized.us

- Created the Full Offer Stack, from a low-ticket entry point to a high-ticket, done-for-you service.

- Wrote Press Releases and News Articles to announce our pivot.

- Developed a Complete Marketing and Implementation Plan, including a full quarter's worth of social media content.

It was an exhilarating, exhausting, and utterly transformative experience. By Monday morning, we didn't just have a rough idea scrawled on a whiteboard. We had a polished, market-ready offer, complete with all the authority assets and promotional materials needed to launch it with a bang.

AI was the engine, but our Category Design was the steering wheel. It gave us the strategic clarity, the creative horsepower, and the operational efficiency to bring a massive vision to life at a speed that would have been impossible just a year prior. If you are wondering if you can truly adapt and thrive in this new world, the answer is an emphatic yes.

The most dangerous place in business is not being incompetent. It's being amazing but forgettable. You don't need to be the smartest person in the room. You just need to own the idea that your market is craving, and then use the awesome power of AI to amplify that idea at a scale that makes you impossible to ignore.

Be the only. Not the best. That is the game.

Summary

The battlefield of modern business is littered with the ghosts of talented experts who made one fatal mistake: they tried to be the best, not the only. In today's AI-driven world, competence has become a commodity. Simply being good at what you do places you in a crowded arena, forcing you into a soul-crushing race to the bottom on price and effort. The escape route is not to hustle harder but to think differently.

This chapter has provided your blueprint for that escape. It demands a conscious evolution from being a mere "Dabbler" with new tools to becoming a "Dominator" of a new domain. This is the path of the Category King. True market dominance isn't found by fighting for a piece of an existing pie; it's found by creating a new one. You do this by carving out a hyper-specific niche you can own, planting your flag with a Big Idea that changes the conversation, and building an unassailable fortress with named, Signature IP that makes your genius tangible. This is how you stop being an option and start being the only logical choice.

Remember, AI is the great amplifier, not the strategist. Without a clear category, it will only amplify your invisibility. But when fused with a powerful, unique position, it becomes the engine that multiplies your influence, turning your singular idea into a ubiquitous presence across books, content, and client-attracting funnels.

The businesses that will define the next decade are not those who sell a generic service, but those who own a category, a powerful idea, and a market position that no one else can replicate. The choice is yours: remain a forgotten expert in a sea of sameness, or step up, claim your category, and become irreplaceable. The time to build your kingdom is now.

Action Items:

1. Identify Your Stage: Be brutally honest with yourself. Are you a Denier, a Dabbler, or a Dominator? Write it down and commit to moving to the next level.

2. Define Your Niche: Dedicate two hours this week to a "Niche Clarity" session. Go through the three questions outlined in this chapter and define your hyper-specific audience and their most painful problem.

3. Name Your Big Idea: What is the flag you want to plant? Brainstorm 20+ potential names for your category or unique philosophy. Don't filter yourself. Just get the ideas out.

4. Draft Your Signature IP: Map out the 3-7 steps of your core process. Give it a powerful, branded name. This is your V1 framework.

5. Craft Your Power Positioning Statement: Use the "I help [who] achieve [transformation] using [unique method]" formula. Write it, refine it, and memorize it. Make it the first sentence of your LinkedIn bio.

6. Commit to Owning It: The window of opportunity to define new categories with AI is wide open right now, but it is closing fast. If you don't claim your category, someone else will. Make the decision today to be the one who owns the conversation.

PART II

BUILDING YOUR AI
AUTHORITY ENGINE

CHAPTER 4

CREATING CONTENT FASTER AND SMARTER

Content is king, but engagement is queen, and the lady rules the house.

–Mari Smith

Now we're going to roll up our sleeves and dive into some real-world ways you can use Artificial Intelligence to not just create content faster, **but also smarter.**

Let's start with one of the first tools we brought into our business: Jasper. We began using Jasper about four years ago when AI content creation was just starting to gain traction. It was like opening a brand-new door. Jasper allowed us to quickly generate content in different voices and styles, giving us the flexibility to test new messaging ideas without spending hours staring at a blank page.

While we don't dive deep into Jasper's latest updates here, what's important is how it became a stepping stone for us. It showed us the real possibility of letting AI lend a hand in creating all kinds of content, blog posts, marketing copy, social media captions, you name it. Now we use ChatGPT, Claude, Gemini, CoPilot, Manus, and more, just to name a few. Just like we mentioned earlier, we took our Tedx talk, articles, podcast episodes and more and turned it into this book using a mixture of these tools.

That early experience taught us a **powerful lesson**: when you partner with AI, you don't just work faster, you work with more creativity, more flexibility, and a whole lot less stress. And that's what we want for you, too!

A powerful tool that can generate a wide variety of content from a single prompt is The Oasis AI. By inputting your book or a simple description of your subject or talking out your idea, The Oasis AI can create numerous outputs, including:

- Social media content, such as Twitter threads and LinkedIn posts. These can be tailored to different platforms for a broader reach.

- Long-form content, like New York Times articles and blog posts. This allows for the rapid creation of substantial written material.

- Presentation outlines, such as TED Talk outlines and pitch decks. This can significantly speed up the initial planning stages of presentations.

- Marketing materials, including email sequences, keywords, and elevator pitches. This streamlines the development of essential marketing communications.

- Creative content, even suggesting song lyrics. This showcases the versatility of the tool beyond standard business content.

Tools like The Oasis AI can even generate a wide array of content, including email sequences and social media posts, from a simple prompt about your business. Imagine the efficiency gained! Now, let me show you in real time.

Once I upload my book or enter the prompt by talking or typing, it instantly creates multiple forms of content such as social media threads, TED Talk outlines, email sequences, and even blog post articles.

The process is remarkably efficient, as demonstrated by the instant generation of diverse content from a brief input about a tour company. **The Oasis AI** offers a way to overcome the need to ask for each content format individually, saving significant time and effort in the content creation workflow. Many of its features are available for free or at a low monthly cost, making it an accessible option.

Prompt: Create a bold and engaging promo for the launch of *Be Recognized: The AI Authority Engine for Experts Who Want to Be Known, Be Profitable, and Be Published* by Melanie Johnson and Jenn Foster, a powerful guide that shows high achieving professionals how to turn their expertise into a brand legacy using AI, strategic content repurposing, and smart visibility systems. The tone should be inspiring, empowering, and slightly disruptive, crafted as a short-form promotional video script or social post (60 seconds or 300 words) targeting entrepreneurs, coaches, consultants, authors, and business leaders who want to stand out in a crowded digital world. Include a strong hook like "You don't need more content. You need more *recognition*," a compelling stat or story about authority and visibility, and a clear transformation, from overlooked expert to industry icon, ending with a strong call to action inviting the audience to get the book, visit the website, or schedule a strategy call. Use hashtags like #BeRecognized #AuthorityEngine #AIForExperts.

Output: the following was copied and pasted without editing from *The Oasis*

Elevate Expertise: Become Industry Icon

TikTok Script

[Opening shot: Energetic music plays. The camera zooms in on a lively host standing against a backdrop of bustling city life, symbolizing the digital world.]

Host: "Hey, world-changers! You don't need more content. You need more recognition! "

[Cut to fast-paced clips of people scrolling through endless social media feeds, looking overwhelmed.]

Host: "Ever feel like your genius is just another drop in the ocean of online noise? You're not alone, and we've got just the life raft! "

[Switch to a dynamic animation of a book titled "Be Recognized: AI Authority Engine" flying into frame.]

Host: "Introducing 'Be Recognized: AI Authority Engine' by the legendary Melanie Johnson and Jenn Foster! This isn't just a book; it's your ultimate playbook to transform from an overlooked expert to an industry icon! "

[Cut to a quick montage of people looking confident and successful after using the book.]

Host: "Imagine turning your expertise into a brand legacy using AI, strategic content repurposing, and smart visibility systems. Sounds like magic, right? But it's not! It's real, and it's waiting for you!"

[Overlay a compelling stat: "Did you know 70% of professionals struggle to get noticed online? Time to flip the script! "]

Host: "With this guide, you'll go from being the best-kept secret to the talk of the town! 🎙️ "

[Cut to a shot of the host holding the book, looking excited.]

Host: "Ready to step into the spotlight and OWN it? 💡 Get your copy now, visit our website, or schedule a strategy call today! Let's make your expertise unforgettable! "

[Closing shot: The host winks at the camera as the screen fills with bold text: "Be Recognized. Be Unforgettable."]

Host: "Remember, you're not just building a brand; you're building a legacy! ✨"

[End screen with hashtags: #BeRecognized #AuthorityEngine #AIForExperts]

[Music fades out]

🚫 BS Filter

"Be Recognized: AI Authority Engine" by Melanie Johnson and Jenn Foster is a guide for professionals to transform their expertise into a brand legacy using AI, strategic content repurposing, and visibility systems.

📝 Blog Post

✦ You don't need more content. You need more recognition. ✦

In the ever-evolving digital landscape, where voices clamor for attention, how do you ensure yours rises above the din? Enter "Be Recognized: AI Authority Engine – Elevating Experts to Industry Icons" by the visionary minds of Melanie Johnson and Jenn Foster. This isn't just another guide; it's your blueprint to transform your expertise into a lasting legacy.

Imagine this: 82% of people trust a company more when its leadership is visible online. Yet, how many experts languish in obscurity, their brilliance overshadowed by the noise? The time has come to change that narrative.

Melanie and Jenn unveil a revolutionary approach that harnesses the power of AI, strategic content repurposing, and smart visibility systems. They empower high-achieving professionals like you to not just participate in the conversation, but to lead it.

Picture your transformation from being just another name in your field to becoming an industry icon, respected, recognized, and revered. With "Be Recognized," you'll learn to amplify your voice, extend your reach, and imprint your expertise indelibly on the world.

This is more than a book; it's a movement. It's about reclaiming your spotlight and becoming the go-to authority in your niche. Are you ready to elevate your brand and make waves in your industry?

Don't let your brilliance go unnoticed. Dive into "Be Recognized" today. Visit our website, grab your copy, or schedule a strategy call now. Join the ranks of industry icons who refuse to be overlooked.

#BeRecognized   #AuthorityEngine   #AIForExperts #IndustryIcon #ElevateYourBrand

The digital world is vast, but your voice is powerful. Let it be heard.

YouTube Script

[Opening shot: A dynamic montage of entrepreneurs, coaches, consultants, authors, and business leaders looking frustrated and overshadowed, interspersed with vibrant clips of crowded digital spaces.]

Narrator (V.O.): "You don't need more content. You need more recognition."

[Cut to a powerful, close-up shot of a determined entrepreneur staring at a screen, then looking up with newfound confidence.]

Narrator (V.O.): "In a world overflowing with noise, how do you stand out? How do you elevate from overlooked expert to an industry icon?"

[Cut to fast-paced visuals of digital noise, endless scrolling through social media, chaotic notifications, and content overload.]

Narrator (V.O.): "The answer isn't more content. It's smarter visibility."

[Transition to a sleek animation of the book cover "Be Recognized: AI Authority Engine" by Melanie Johnson and Jenn Foster.]

Narrator (V.O.): "Introducing 'Be Recognized: AI Authority Engine', your ultimate guide to transforming expertise into a lasting brand legacy."

[Cut to engaging shots of Melanie Johnson and Jenn Foster passionately speaking to a captivated audience.]

Melanie Johnson (V.O.): "We've harnessed the power of AI and strategic content repurposing to turn recognition into your superpower."

Jenn Foster (V.O.): "With the right systems, you can break through the digital clutter and become an authority in your field."

[Cut to a statistic on screen: "Did you know 70% of entrepreneurs feel unnoticed despite their expertise?"]

Narrator (V.O.): "Don't be just another expert. Be the icon your industry looks up to."

[Transition to an inspiring transformation montage: individuals standing on stages, being interviewed, and receiving recognition as industry leaders.]

Narrator (V.O.): "Unlock the secrets to becoming unforgettable. Elevate your brand, amplify your influence, and leave a legacy."

[Cut to a clear call to action with the book cover and website URL: "Get your copy now at [website URL]. Transform your recognition. Transform your life."]

[Ending shot: The book on a pedestal with hashtags on screen.]

Narrator (V.O.): "Visit our website, grab your copy, or schedule a strategy call today. #BeRecognized #AuthorityEngine #AIForExperts"

[Fade out with a powerful, uplifting musical crescendo.]

Outline

I. Introduction

  A. Hook

    1. "You don't need more content. You need more recognition."

II. The Challenge

  A. Overwhelming digital noise

  B. Struggle for visibility

III. The Solution

A. Introduction of Be Recognized: AI Authority Engine

1. Authors: Melanie Johnson and Jenn Foster

2. Guide for elevating experts to industry icons

IV. Key Strategies

A. AI Integration

1. Leveraging AI for personal branding

B. Strategic Content Repurposing

1. Maximizing existing content

C. Smart Visibility Systems

1. Enhancing presence in digital spaces

V. Transformation

A. From Overlooked Expert

B. To Industry Icon

VI. Compelling Story or Statistic

A. Example of authority and visibility success

VII. Call to Action

A. Get the book

B. Visit the website

C. Schedule a strategy call

VIII. Conclusion

A. Empowering message

1. Encouragement to stand out

B. Hashtags

1. #BeRecognized

2. #AuthorityEngine

3. #AIForExperts

💬 Text Message

Hey there! 🚀 Ready to elevate your brand to legendary status? Check out "Be Recognized: AI Authority Engine" by Melanie Johnson and Jenn Foster. This powerful guide is your ticket from being just another expert to an industry icon. ⭐

"You don't need more content. You need more recognition." With AI, strategic content repurposing, and smart visibility systems, transform your expertise into a lasting brand legacy. Did you know 90% of experts are overlooked online? Don't be one of them.

Get ready to stand out in the digital crowd. Grab your copy now, visit our site, or schedule a strategy call. It's time to own your authority! 💪

#BeRecognized #AuthorityEngine #AIForExperts

🐦 Twitter Thread

1/5 🚀 "You don't need more content. You need more recognition." Dive into 'Be Recognized: AI Authority Engine' by Melanie Johnson & Jenn Foster. Transform expertise into a brand legacy. Elevate from overlooked expert to industry icon. #BeRecognized #AuthorityEngine

2/5 💡 Did you know 70% of professionals feel their potential isn't fully recognized? It's time to change that narrative. Discover how AI, strategic content repurposing, and visibility systems can revolutionize your brand. #AIForExperts #BeRecognized

3/5 🔥 Entrepreneurs, coaches, and leaders: The digital world is crowded, but your voice deserves to rise above it. 'Be Recognized' offers the roadmap to making your expertise unmistakable. Don't blend in, stand out. #AuthorityEngine #BeRecognized

4/5 ✍ From overlooked to iconic: Transform your professional landscape with insights from 'Be Recognized.' Elevate your authority and leave a lasting legacy in your industry. Ready to be an icon? #AIForExperts #AuthorityEngine

5/5 📖 Ready to take the leap? Get 'Be Recognized: AI Authority Engine' today. Visit our website or schedule a strategy call to start your journey from expert to icon. Your legacy awaits. #BeRecognized #AIForExperts #AuthorityEngine

Elevator Pitch

Introducing "Be Recognized: AI Authority Engine" by Melanie Johnson and Jenn Foster—a transformative guide that elevates high-achieving professionals into industry icons. This book unveils the secrets to turning your expertise into a lasting brand legacy through the power of AI, strategic content repurposing, and smart visibility systems. Whether you're a seasoned expert or emerging leader, "Be Recognized" empowers you to harness cutting-edge tools and techniques to amplify your influence and leave an indelible mark in your field. Get ready to elevate your brand and become the authority you were meant to be.

📧 Professional Email

Subject: Elevate Your Expertise with "Be Recognized: AI Authority Engine"

Dear [Recipient's Name],

I hope this message finds you well. I'm excited to introduce "Be Recognized: AI Authority Engine – Elevating Experts to Industry Icons" by Melanie Johnson and Jenn Foster. This guide is designed to transform high-achieving professionals into recognized industry leaders.

Key Message: You don't need more content. You need more recognition.

In today's digital landscape, authority is crucial. Research shows that 70% of consumers are more likely to trust a brand with a recognized expert at the helm. With this book, you will learn how to leverage AI, repurpose strategic content, and implement smart visibility systems to build a lasting brand legacy.

Transformation: Transition from being an overlooked expert to an industry icon. This book provides the tools and insights necessary to achieve that status.

Call to Action: To stand out in a crowded digital world, I invite you to explore this transformative guide. Get your copy, visit our website, or schedule a strategy call today.

Join the movement and redefine your professional journey.

Best regards,

[Your Name]

[Your Contact Information]

#BeRecognized #AuthorityEngine #AIForExperts

Keywords

AI Authority Engine, brand legacy, expertise, industry icons, strategic content repurposing, smart visibility systems, Melanie Johnson and Jenn Foster

👻💼 LinkedIn Post

👽 You don't need more content. You need more recognition. 👽

In a world overflowing with noise, simply shouting louder isn't the answer. It's about being heard by the right people, at the right time. Imagine transforming from an overlooked expert into an industry icon, commanding respect and recognition with every word.

Introducing "Be Recognized: AI Authority Engine" by Melanie Johnson and Jenn Foster, a game-changing guide that empowers high-achieving professionals to elevate their expertise into a brand legacy. This isn't just a book; it's your blueprint to becoming the go-to authority in your field.

Consider this: 92% of consumers trust individuals over brands. Yet, so many experts remain hidden in the shadows. What if you could harness the power of AI, strategic content repurposing, and smart visibility systems to shine brighter than ever before?

This is your moment. With cutting-edge strategies and insights, "Be Recognized" offers a clear roadmap to transform your knowledge into influence, your influence into impact, and your impact into a lasting legacy.

Whether you're an entrepreneur, coach, consultant, author, or business leader, this is your invitation to step into the spotlight. Are you ready to leave obscurity behind and embrace your destiny as an industry icon?

Don't just be another voice in the crowd. Be recognized. 🌟

📸 Get your copy now, visit our website, or schedule your strategy call today. Let's embark on this transformative journey together.

#BeRecognized #AuthorityEngine #AIForExperts #IndustryIcon #VisibilityRevolution

◈ NY Times Article

New York Times Exclusive: Transforming Expertise into Influence with AI

In a digital era where noise drowns out nuance, "Be Recognized: AI Authority Engine" emerges as the definitive guide for those determined not just to be heard, but to be unforgettable. Written by visionary authors Melanie Johnson and Jenn Foster, this groundbreaking work offers a lifeline to high achievers desperate to transform their hard-earned expertise into a lasting brand legacy.

"You don't need more content. You need more recognition."

In a startling revelation, studies show that 70% of professionals struggle to leverage their expertise into meaningful visibility. But what if the key to standing out isn't creating more, but being seen more strategically?

Johnson and Foster unveil a roadmap to elevate overlooked experts into industry icons. Through the innovative use of AI, strategic content repurposing, and savvy visibility systems, this book promises a metamorphosis: from being just another voice in the crowd to becoming the go-to authority in your field.

Picture this: You, the once-faded expert, now commanding the stage with a presence that demands respect and admiration. This isn't just about fame, it's about influence, impact, and leaving a legacy.

The time to step into your spotlight is now. Are you ready to harness the power of AI and strategic insight to redefine your career?

Take the first step towards your transformation. Get your copy of "Be Recognized: AI Authority Engine" today. Visit [website link] or schedule your personalized strategy call now.

Because in a world that's content-rich but recognition-poor, the true currency is authority.

#BeRecognized #AuthorityEngine #AIForExperts

Dare to be more than just another expert. Dare to be iconic.

✍ "The Oasis" Summary

🎥 You don't need more content. You need more recognition. Imagine transforming from an unseen expert to an industry icon. 🔍 In the crowded digital landscape, standing out isn't optional; it's essential. Introducing *Be Recognized: AI Authority Engine* by Melanie Johnson and Jenn Foster, your blueprint to elevate your expertise into a brand legacy.

🔍 Did you know that 70% of professionals feel their skills are overlooked in their field? This ends now. Dive into a guide that harnesses the power of AI, strategic content repurposing, and smart visibility systems to amplify your presence. 📝

💡 *Be Recognized* isn't just a book; it's your key to unlocking unparalleled authority. Whether you're an entrepreneur, coach, consultant, author, or business leader, this is your moment to rise above the noise and be seen as the go-to expert in your industry.

🔥 Get ready for a transformation, from being the best-kept secret to becoming the face of your field. It's time to disrupt the status quo and build a legacy that lasts.

🎯 Don't let your expertise go unnoticed. Grab your copy now, visit our website, or schedule a strategy call today. Step into your power and be recognized. ✴

#BeRecognized #AuthorityEngine #AIForExperts

End of "The Oasis" Content

That was a strong draft with lots of emojis. Remember, this output is the first draft. Now it's your job to edit and refine the text. Editing the text, emoji's, em-dashes, etc will make sure it doesn't look like AI wrote it. Never copy and paste the content without editing it first. We share this custom GPT, *Un-AI Your AI Writing*, as a bonus. Visit our website to access the bonus.

BeRecognized.us/book

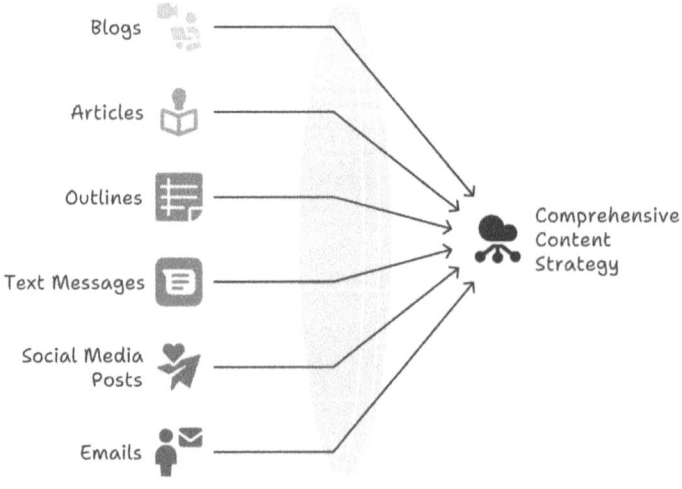

Unified Content Creation

Custom GPT's

Let's discuss custom GPTs. Have you heard of ChatGPT? ChatGPT is a conversational AI chatbot developed by OpenAI. It's designed to understand and generate human-like text, allowing it to engage in conversations, answer questions, and create various forms of content. Essentially, it's a powerful language model that can be used for a wide range of tasks, from answering questions to generating creative text formats. Now a Custom GPT is just like it says CUSTOM. These allow you to create specialized AI models tailored to your unique needs and content. A Custom GPT is a specialized version of OpenAI's Generative Pre-trained Transformer (GPT) models, specifically designed and fine-tuned for a particular purpose or task. Think of it as creating a personalized chatbot built on the robust foundation of ChatGPT, but with specific knowledge, instructions, and even actions. By training a custom GPT with your own content, such as books, videos, and speeches, it can learn to write in your specific tone of voice and style. This effectively allows you to "clone yourself" in the AI space for content creation.

Here's how custom GPTs can be particularly useful:

- **Generating personalized communications:** You can use a custom GPT trained on your previous communications to draft email replies that sound authentically like you, even incorporating some of the recipient's language.

- **Creating content aligned with your brand:** By uploading all your brand materials into a custom GPT, you can ensure that all generated content consistently reflects your brand's voice and messaging.

- **Assisting with content repurposing:** A custom GPT could potentially be used to rephrase or adapt existing content in your specific style for different platforms.

- **Streamlining workflows:** Creating projects within platforms like ChatGPT allows you to save specific data and prompts related to different authors or business areas, making it easier to manage and generate content for various needs.

The ability to create a custom GPT that speaks and writes like you can significantly enhance the speed and efficiency of content creation while maintaining your unique personal or brand voice. This level of personalization goes beyond standard AI models, offering a powerful way to generate content that truly resonates with your audience.

In conclusion, AI tools like The Oasis AI and custom GPTs have opened up a whole new world when it comes to creating content faster and smarter. One tool we love using is ChatHub. This tool uses more than one AI at a time. You can connect six or more AIs to see what the output is from not only ChatGPT, but Gemini, Claude, and more. It enables you to evaluate different AI outputs for the same prompt.

Using AI could help you generate content in different styles and voices. Using The Oasis AI makes it even easier to whip up all kinds of content formats from just a few simple prompts. With custom GPTs, you can create highly personalized content that sounds just like *you*, your voice, your style, your message.

When you use these tools strategically, you're not just saving time, you're supercharging your ability to communicate clearly, build deeper connections with your audience, and establish yourself as the go-to authority in your niche.

So don't be afraid to dive in. The future of content creation is here, and it's ready for you to take full advantage of it!

Let me share a couple of real-life stories that show just how powerful AI tools can be when it comes to creating content that truly *sounds like you* and elevates your brand presence.

We had one client, Bob, who wanted to take his email marketing to the next level. Now, if you've ever written emails for someone else, you know it's not just about the words; it's about *capturing their voice,* their tone, and their personality. So what did we do? We created a custom GPT just for him. We trained it on his previous emails, his speaking style, and even his social media posts.

The result? Emails started flowing out that sounded exactly like he had written them himself. His warmth, his humor, even his little turns of phrase were right there. His audience couldn't tell the difference, and better yet, his engagement rates shot up because people felt like they were getting a real, personal message from him every time. It was like having him sit down for coffee with every single subscriber on his list.

Then we had another amazing project where we worked with our client Kristin, who wanted to really boost her marketing across the board, her website, her blog, LinkedIn articles, and even her YouTube channel.

We brought in The Oasis AI to help get it done, and let me tell you, it was a game-changer. With just a few simple prompts, Oasis helped us generate tons of smart, polished content that stayed true to her brand and expertise. We turned around a full series of blog posts, LinkedIn articles that started real conversations, and YouTube video scripts that made her content strategy feel effortless.

And the best part? She wasn't bogged down spending hours creating all this herself. She stayed focused on her zone of genius while we made sure her voice was out there consistently, building authority and attracting new clients.

These experiences show just how transformational the right AI tools can be, not just in saving time, but in creating real, authentic communication that connects and converts.

Meet Your Mini-Me – Using AI to Multiply Your Message

Let's talk about something really fun: making a "mini-you" with AI. Now, don't worry, we're not cloning anyone in a lab! This is about creating a little digital version of you that can help you with your business, your brand, or even your everyday tasks.

Here's the idea: you take a tool like ChatGPT or Delphi, and you teach it how you talk. You give it your writing, maybe some videos or voice memos, and it starts to learn your style. What words you use. How you explain things. Even the way you make people feel.

And what happens next? You've got a smart assistant that sounds just like you and can help get things done. Pretty amazing, right?

Let's break down how you can use your mini-me:

1. **Answering Questions for Your Audience**

   If you're getting the same questions all the time, about your work, your book, or your services, your AI clone can help answer them just like you would. Brendon Burchard, a top performance coach, does this with his audience. His AI answers questions in his voice, so more people can get support even when he's busy.

2. **Creating Content While You Sleep**

   Whether it's writing a newsletter, a video script, or a post for Instagram, your mini-you can get the ball rolling. You give it an idea, and it gives you a first draft. You still add your personal touch, but the hard part is already done. Brendon uses this to create motivational messages, blogs, and even outline speeches.

3. **Teaching or Coaching in More Places**

   Your AI mini-me can help people learn from you, even when you're off doing something else. It can guide your clients through your programs, remind them of key lessons, or give tips that sound just like you. That's what Brendon's doing; he's letting people get access to his knowledge through his AI, anytime they need it.

Here's why I love this: it helps you help more people, without stretching yourself too thin. It gives you time back. It lets your voice reach further.

And most of all, it's not about replacing you. It's about multiplying you. So your heart, your message, and your magic go even further.

So if you've ever thought, "I wish I could be in two places at once," now you can with a little help from your AI mini-me.

Summary

AI isn't just about creating more content; it's about creating smarter, more authentic content faster than ever before. Early tools like Jasper opened the door to AI-assisted writing, but today, platforms like The Oasis AI and custom GPTs allow entrepreneurs to generate entire ecosystems of content, tailored exactly to their voice and brand. By strategically using AI to brainstorm ideas, produce diverse content formats, and replicate your personal style, you can massively scale your visibility, deepen audience trust, and stay consistently top-of-mind, all without adding more hours to your workload.

Action Items

1. Choose one AI tool (such as The Oasis AI or a custom GPT) and use it to create a new piece of content this week.

2. Train a custom GPT using your emails, blog posts, or recorded talks to clone your voice and style for future content.

3. Create a batch of content from one simple prompt (social posts, emails, or blog drafts) to experience the speed and flexibility of AI-assisted creation.

4. Identify one key content channel (email list, LinkedIn, YouTube) where you will consistently publish AI-supported, brand-aligned material.

5. Focus on quality and authenticity by reviewing and personalizing AI-generated drafts to ensure they sound true to your voice.

CHAPTER 5

AUTOMATING SALES
AND CUSTOMER COMMUNICATION

The secret of change is to focus all of your energy not on fighting the old, but on building the new.

–Socrates

Let's be honest for a moment. What does the "old" way of running your business really feel like? It's that Sunday evening dread, a knot tightening in your stomach as you anticipate opening your inbox. It's the constant, nagging feeling that a critical lead has fallen through the cracks. It's the memory of that fantastic sales call you had on Tuesday, but the crucial follow-up email you were supposed to send is still a half-written draft, now buried under a mountain of new, urgent fires.

The old way is spending your most creative hours, the hours you should be dedicating to strategy, innovation, and building relationships, on monotonous, repetitive, administrative tasks. It's the manual follow-ups, the scheduling back-and-forth, the frantic search for call notes, and the impossible task of giving every single customer the personal attention they deserve. You're trapped in a state of perpetual reaction, a firefighter armed with a leaky bucket, dashing from one blaze to the next. You built a business to create freedom, yet you've inadvertently constructed a prison of your own manual processes.

If this sounds even remotely familiar, I want you to take a deep breath and internalize the wisdom of Socrates. The solution is not to fight this chaotic reality, to hustle harder, or to work longer hours. That is a battle you will never win. The solution is to focus all of your energy on building the new.

Achieving High-Value Strategy with AI

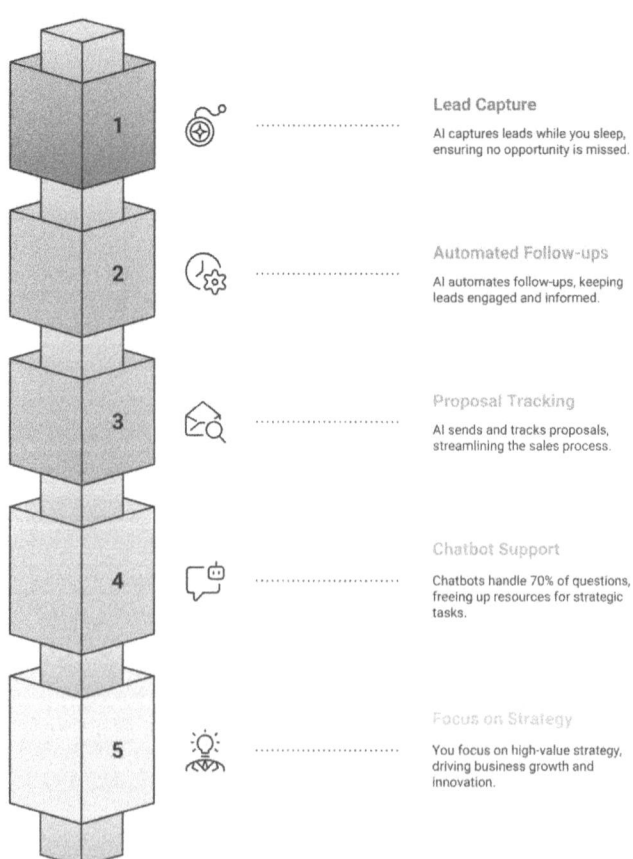

Lead Capture
AI captures leads while you sleep, ensuring no opportunity is missed.

Automated Follow-ups
AI automates follow-ups, keeping leads engaged and informed.

Proposal Tracking
AI sends and tracks proposals, streamlining the sales process.

Chatbot Support
Chatbots handle 70% of questions, freeing up resources for strategic tasks.

Focus on Strategy
You focus on high-value strategy, driving business growth and innovation.

Welcome to the new way. Welcome to the Frictionless Firm. In this new paradigm, we leverage Artificial Intelligence not as a simple tool, but as a strategic partner. We build an intelligent, automated engine that works tirelessly for you in the background, 24 hours a day, 7 days a week. It's an engine that nurtures leads with perfect consistency, ensures no opportunity is ever missed, and empowers you to deliver a customer experience so personal and responsive it feels like magic.

This chapter is your blueprint for building that engine. We will move beyond the theoretical and dive deep into the practical, step-by-step systems that will fundamentally transform two of the most critical, and traditionally time-consuming, functions of your business: sales and customer communication.

The Mindset Shift: From Manual Hustle to Intelligent Automation

Before we touch a single tool, we must address the most important component: your mindset. For decades, the entrepreneurial ethos has been dominated by "hustle culture." The prevailing wisdom was that success was a direct result of brute force: more calls, more emails, more hours at the desk. The entrepreneur was the hero who could outwork everyone else.

AI renders that entire philosophy obsolete.

The new currency of success is not manual effort; it is strategic design. The hero is no longer the person who can juggle the most tasks, but the one who can design the most intelligent systems. This requires a profound shift from being the primary doer in your business to becoming the primary architect. Your job is no longer to turn the crank, but to build the machine that turns itself.

This transition is about reclaiming your most precious and finite resource: your cognitive load. Every minute you spend remembering to send a follow-up email is a minute you don't spend thinking about a new marketing angle. Every ounce of mental energy you expend on scheduling is energy you can't use to solve a complex client problem. AI's greatest promise is not just time savings; it's the liberation of your mental bandwidth. It automates the low-level, administrative thinking to free you up for the high-level, strategic, and creative thinking that only you can do.

Think of AI as a "cyborg" extension of your own mind. It has a perfect memory, flawless consistency, and infinite patience for repetitive tasks. Your role is to infuse it with your wisdom, your strategy, and your personality. You build the new, and then it works for you, creating a business that is not only more profitable but also profoundly more sustainable and enjoyable to run.

Part 1: The AI-Powered Sales Engine

Let's dissect the traditional sales funnel and rebuild it, piece by piece, with intelligent automation. Our goal is to create a system that qualifies, nurtures, and engages leads with such precision and personalization that by the time you, the human, get involved, the prospect is already warm, educated, and predisposed to say "yes."

Stage 1: Top of Funnel - Lead Generation and Intelligent Qualification

The old way involved manually sifting through leads, making educated guesses about who was most interested, and wasting countless hours on prospects who were never a good fit.

The new way uses AI to do this with scientific precision.

The 24/7 AI Concierge: Imagine a chatbot on your website that does more than just say, "How can I help you?" Imagine it's been trained on all your past client interactions and sales scripts. It can engage visitors in real-time, ask intelligent qualifying questions ("What's the biggest challenge you're facing with X right now?" or "What's the approximate size of your team?"), and even book qualified leads directly onto your calendar, all while you sleep.

AI-Driven Lead Scoring: Tools can now integrate with your website and CRM to automatically score leads based on their behavior. Someone who visits your pricing page, downloads a case study, and watches a webinar is a much "hotter" lead than someone who just reads a single blog post. AI can track these signals, assign a score, and alert you or trigger an automated sequence only when a lead's score crosses a certain threshold. This ensures you focus your precious manual effort exclusively on those who have demonstrated real intent.

Hyper-Personalized Outreach at Scale: Forget the generic email blasts of the past. AI allows for a new level of personalization. By scraping a prospect's LinkedIn profile and company website, AI can help you draft outreach emails that reference their specific role, recent company news, or shared connections. Tools like Clay.com are pioneering this space, allowing you to build highly targeted lead lists and automate outreach that feels genuinely one-to-one.

Stage 2: Middle of Funnel - The AI-Assisted Conversation & Nurturing

This is where most sales are won or lost, in the follow-up. It's also where entrepreneurs, juggling a million other tasks, most often drop the ball. This is where AI becomes your sales-execution superstar.

The Perfect Sales Call (and Flawless Follow-up): I've personally seen a massive transformation in my own sales workflow by building a system around this. It starts with a tool like Fathom or Otter.ai. During any online meeting, the AI listens, records, and transcribes the entire conversation in real-time. The moment the call ends, I have a full video recording, a searchable transcript, and, most importantly, an AI-generated summary of the key points and action items.

But here's where the real magic happens. I take that summary and transcript and feed it into a custom GPT that I've trained on my specific communication style, my core frameworks, and my past successful emails.

My prompt looks something like this:

Prompt: "Act as my expert sales assistant, with a friendly, confident, and consultative tone. Attached is the AI summary and full transcript from a sales call with [Prospect Name] of [Company Name]. Please do the following:

- Draft a warm, compelling follow-up email.
- The subject line should be engaging and reference our conversation.
- The opening should build rapport by referencing a specific personal or business point we connected on.
- The body of the email must summarize the prospect's primary challenges using their own words and phrases from the transcript.
- Connect their challenges to the key value propositions of my solution that we discussed.
- Clearly outline the specific next steps we agreed upon.
- Keep the email concise and easy to read."

Within 60 seconds, I have a near-perfect draft. It's written in my voice, but it's enhanced with a perfect memory of the conversation, incorporating the prospect's own language. This creates a powerful psychological effect: the prospect feels deeply heard and understood. All I need to do is a quick final polish (the final 10% human touch) and hit send. This process has reduced my follow-up time from 30 minutes of painful, brain-draining work to less than three minutes of simple review.

The Intelligent Proposal & Automated Persistence: After sending a proposal, the dreaded "follow-up black hole" begins. AI completely eliminates this. Using any modern CRM or email marketing tool (like HubSpot, ActiveCampaign, or even Mailchimp), you can create automated email sequences that are triggered by prospect engagement. This is not a generic "just checking in" blast; it's an intelligent, branching workflow.

Scenario 1: Proposal is NOT Opened.

- Day 3: Automated Email 1: "Hi [First Name], just wanted to make sure my proposal didn't get buried. Let me know if you have any initial questions!"

- Day 7: Automated Email 2: "Hi [First Name], circling back one last time on the proposal I sent. Happy to walk you through it if that would be helpful."

Scenario 2: Proposal IS Opened, but No Reply.

- Day 2: Automated Email 1: "Hi [First Name], great to see you had a chance to look at the proposal. I'd love to hear your initial thoughts when you have a moment."

- Day 5: Automated Email 2: "Hi [First Name], I know you're busy, but I'm really excited about how we could help you [achieve specific goal discussed]. Did the section on [mention specific part of the proposal] resonate with you?"

Scenario 3: High Engagement (Opened 5+ times, links clicked).

- Immediate Action: This doesn't trigger an email. It triggers an internal notification directly to you via Slack or email: "AI ALERT: [Prospect Name] is highly engaged with the proposal. Now is the perfect time for a personal phone call."

This system ensures perfect, polite persistence without you ever having to remember who to follow up with and when. It runs 24/7, ensuring no lead ever goes cold due to simple neglect.

Stage 3: Bottom of Funnel - Frictionless Closing and Onboarding

The final stage of the sale should be smooth and seamless, building excitement and confidence for your new client.

Automated Contract Generation: Once a prospect says "yes," tools can automatically generate a contract or agreement, pre-filled with their information, and send it out for e-signature via platforms like PandaDoc or DocuSign.

AI-Powered Personalized Onboarding: Imagine your new client receives a welcome email with a short video. But it's not a generic video. It's a video of you (or your AI avatar) saying, "Hi [Client Name], I'm so excited to start working with you to solve [specific problem they mentioned] and help you achieve [specific goal they mentioned]." Tools like Synthesia or HeyGen make this personalized video generation at scale a reality, creating an unforgettable first impression.

Seamless Team Handover: AI can summarize the key promises, client goals, and communication notes from the entire sales process and automatically create a project brief for your delivery or customer success team. This ensures a smooth transition and that the client never has to repeat themselves, feeling cared for from the very first moment.

Your Book: The Silent Salesperson That Works 24/7

Imagine having a top-performing salesperson, one who never sleeps, never takes a vacation, and always delivers your message perfectly.

They know your voice. They understand your audience. They articulate your offer better than most of your team. They can warm up cold leads, close warm ones, and position you as the go-to authority in your space, all without ever needing to be micromanaged.

That's what a well-written business book does.

It's your silent salesperson, and it's working even when you're not.

Your book doesn't just sit on a shelf or live on Amazon. It's a living asset. A lead magnet. A credibility builder. A trust accelerator. And in the right hands (or inbox), it's often the tipping point between "I'm curious" and "I'm in."

How Your Book Attracts Leads

It Pre-Qualifies and Pre-Sells

A good book filters your audience. The right people will self-identify with your message and your frameworks. The wrong ones will opt out, and that's a good thing. By the time someone finishes your book (or even the first few chapters), they either "get it" or they don't. You'll spend less time explaining and more time enrolling.

It Creates Instant Authority

If your competitors have a website and a podcast, but you have a book, you win. A book creates a perception of depth, legitimacy, and thought leadership. In a world of throwaway content, a published book signals: "I have something to say, and I've organized it into a system."

It Generates Referrals

People love to gift, recommend, or forward books. A client might share your book with a peer. A podcast host might read it and invite you to speak. A conference organizer may read your framework and reach out to have you train their team. Books travel, and they open doors as they go.

It Powers Your Lead Magnets

Use your book to offer a free chapter, a book-based quiz, or a "Book + Strategy Call" funnel. It's the perfect low-friction offer that leads to high-conversion conversations.

How Your Book Closes Deals

It Becomes Your Sales Script

Once your methodology is published in book form, it becomes the script for how you sell your services. Your sales calls don't start with "What do you do?" They start with "I read your book and I'm ready for the next step."

It Shortens the Sales Cycle

Clients who read your book arrive more educated, more aligned, and more trusting. You're no longer selling from scratch; you're simply helping them take action on a transformation they already understand.

It Establishes the Value of Your Offer

Your book demonstrates your process, your case studies, and the stakes of not solving the problem. It reframes your price as a smart investment in the outcome your book has already walked them through.

It Makes You the Obvious Choice

When a prospect is deciding between you and three other service providers, and you're the only one with a published book that speaks directly to their pain point? You win the deal before the sales call even happens.

Bottom Line

A book is the only marketing asset that educates, qualifies, nurtures, and closes, without needing your constant input.

It doesn't get tired. It doesn't require ad spend. And it doesn't need a follow-up reminder.

It just keeps showing up, building trust, and making you the most recognizable, referable, and credible voice in your space.

If you want to scale your sales, scale your visibility, and scale your impact, start by scaling your ideas into a book that does the heavy lifting for you.

Case Study: Sarah the Consultant's "Frictionless Firm"

Sarah, a brilliant marketing consultant, was a classic case of being a victim of her own success. She was incredible at her craft, but was drowning in the administration of her business. She was working 60-hour weeks, with at least half that time spent on non-billable sales and admin tasks. Leads were falling through the cracks, and her growth had plateaued.

We worked with her to build an AI-Powered Sales Engine. Here's what it looked like:

- Her Website Chatbot: We trained a chatbot, an AI tool called Tidio on her top 20 FAQs, her case studies, and her qualification criteria. The bot now handles 70% of initial website inquiries, answering basic questions and booking qualified leads into "Discovery Sessions" on her calendar.

- Her Fathom + ChatGPT Workflow: She implemented the exact meeting-to-follow-up system described above. This alone saved her 5-7 hours per week and led to a 30% increase in prospects responding positively to her follow-ups because they felt so well understood.

- Her HubSpot Proposal Sequences: We built out the branching follow-up logic in her HubSpot CRM. She no longer lives in fear of forgetting to follow up. The system runs with perfect persistence, and she only gets involved when a prospect replies or when the AI alerts her to a highly engaged lead.

- The Result: Six months later, Sarah's revenue had increased by 40%. But more importantly, she had reclaimed over 20 hours per week. She was no longer a frantic firefighter. She was the calm, confident architect of a thriving business. She had stopped fighting the old and had built the new.

Part 2: The Proactive Customer Communication Engine

Acquiring a new customer is expensive. Losing one due to poor communication is a tragedy. The traditional model of customer service is reactive, waiting for a problem to arise and then trying to fix it. The AI-powered model is proactive; it's about creating a system that anticipates needs, provides instant support, and fosters a community of delighted customers who feel constantly cared for.

The 24/7 Instant Support Agent

The foundation of modern customer communication is an AI chatbot trained on your own knowledge base. This is not the frustrating "I don't understand" bot of five years ago. Modern tools like Intercom, Zendesk AI, or Chatbase can be fed your entire library of help docs, tutorials, FAQs, and even past successful support ticket resolutions.

The Benefit: Over 80% of customer questions are repetitive. Your AI can provide instant, accurate answers to these questions, 24/7. This delivers immediate gratification for your customer and dramatically reduces the ticket volume for your human team. This frees up your people to focus on the complex, nuanced, or high-empathy issues where a human touch is most valuable. It transforms your support team from reactive ticket-takers into proactive customer success advocates.

The AI-Powered "Sixth Sense": Proactive Sentiment Analysis

Imagine you could know a customer was unhappy before they complained or canceled. AI gives you this superpower. By scanning all incoming customer communications, support tickets, emails, community posts, and even social media mentions, AI can perform sentiment analysis in real-time.

How it Works: You can set up rules that trigger alerts based on sentiment. For example: "If a customer with a lifetime value over $5,000 expresses negative sentiment in two or more communications within a 30-day period, create a high-priority task for their designated Customer Success Manager to personally call them within 24 hours." This is like having an early warning system for customer churn, allowing you to intervene and save relationships before they reach a breaking point.

Personalized Nurturing and Education at Scale

A great customer experience isn't just about solving problems; it's about helping customers achieve their goals. AI can monitor how customers are using your product or service and trigger helpful, automated communications.

- Onboarding & Feature Adoption: "Hi [Customer Name], our AI noticed you just used Feature X for the first time! That's awesome. Here's a 2-minute pro-tip video to help you get even more value from it."

- Re-engagement: "Hi [Customer Name], we see you haven't logged into your portal in the last 14 days. We miss you! Is there anything we can help with? Here's a link to our latest case study on how companies like yours are achieving [Goal]."

- Celebrating Wins: "Hi [Customer Name], congratulations! Our system shows you just hit a major milestone by [e.g., creating your 100th design]. We're celebrating with you! Here's a small gift/discount on your next month as a thank you."

These small, personalized, and timely touchpoints create a powerful sense of an ongoing, attentive relationship, dramatically increasing customer loyalty and lifetime value.

The Elephant in the Room: Will AI Replace Human Connection?

There is a common fear that permeates every conversation about automation: "If I automate my communication, won't I lose the human touch that makes my brand special?"

This is a valid fear, but it is based on a fundamental misunderstanding of AI's proper role. AI, when used correctly, does not replace human connection; it creates more space for it.

Think about it. What erodes human connection? A forgotten follow-up. A delayed response to an urgent question. A generic, one-size-fits-all email. These are the symptoms of a human who is overwhelmed by manual, administrative tasks.

AI automates the impersonal so that you can personalize the personal. It handles the scheduling, the reminders, the first drafts, and the basic questions, freeing up your time, energy, and mental space for the moments that truly matter:

- The strategic brainstorming session with a key client.
- The personal phone call to a prospect who the AI identified as highly engaged.
- The thoughtful, empathetic response to a customer facing a complex challenge.
- The time to simply think, create, and innovate.

Summary

Revisit the "10-80-10" rule. You provide the initial 10% of strategic insight. The AI does 80% of the mechanical heavy lifting. Then you come back in to provide the final 10% of human polish, personality, and empathy. The goal is not to automate your humanity; it's to automate the friction that gets in the way of your humanity.

The Frictionless Firm isn't a cold, robotic enterprise. It's a business where technology handles the mundane, allowing the humans at its core to be more strategic, more creative, and more connected than ever before. It's time to stop fighting the old way. It's time to build anew.

Don't just work harder in sales and communication, work smarter. Harness AI to build a sales machine that works for you endlessly, with precision, care, and heart. Your time is your most valuable asset. Reclaim it. Supercharge your revenue. Build relationships that last. And enjoy the freedom of automation.

The future is bright, and it's time to shine!

Action Items: Your 7-Day Plan to a More Frictionless Business

Let's turn these concepts into immediate action. Commit to this one-week sprint.

- Day 1: Get Your "Second Brain." Sign up for a free trial of an AI meeting recorder like Fathom. Connect it to your Zoom or Google Meet and let it run on your next sales or client call.

- Day 2: Run Your First "Magic Follow-Up." Take the transcript and summary from yesterday's call and use ChatGPT with the detailed prompt provided in this chapter. Experience for yourself how fast you can create a superior follow-up email.

- Day 3: Map Your Follow-Up Black Hole. Whiteboard your current process for following up on proposals. Be honest. Where are the leaks? What steps are manual?

- Day 4-5: Write Your First Sequence. Based on your map, write the copy for a simple, 3-email automated sequence for prospects who open your proposal but don't reply. Just write the copy in a Google Doc.

- Day 6: Research Your AI Concierge. Spend 60 minutes exploring one AI chatbot solution like Tidio, Chatbase, or Intercom. Watch their demo videos. Understand what's possible.

- Day 7: Identify Your Proactive Win. Look through your last 10 customer support emails. Find one simple, common question. Now imagine an AI answering that question instantly for your next customer. How much time would that save you over a year?

CHAPTER 6

THE BOOK THAT BUILDS
AN EMPIRE

You're either remarkable or invisible. Make a choice.

—Seth Godin

If you think writing a book has to take months, or even years, you're about to have your mind blown. Jenn and I recently wrote an entire book in just one weekend. That's right, **one weekend!** It's actually this book you are reading right now. We took a transcript from a speech, layered in slides from a presentation, added our bios, wove in real stories about what we've learned and accomplished, and created brand-new content focused on how to *Be Recognized* as an expert in your field. It came together like magic, but let me be clear: this wasn't luck. We've been helping clients do this for years through our VIP Book Creation Days, where in just one day, we can map out, structure, and write most of a book. When you have a system, when you have a vision, and when you take action, you can build an empire with your book faster than you ever dreamed possible. And guess what? If we can do it, you can too!

In the business world, authoring a book has long been a hallmark of thought leadership. A well-crafted book can:

- **Enhance Credibility:** Position yourself as an expert in your field.
- **Expand Reach:** Introduce your ideas to a broader audience.
- **Generate Opportunities:** Lead to speaking engagements, partnerships, and new clients.

However, the traditional process of writing and publishing a book is often time-consuming and resource-intensive. This is where Artificial Intelligence (AI) becomes a game-changer.

Leveraging AI to Streamline the Writing Process

AI tools have revolutionized the way books are written, making the process more efficient and accessible:

- **Content Generation:** Platforms like ChatGPT and Claude can assist in drafting chapters based on prompts, helping to overcome writer's block and maintain a consistent writing schedule.
- **Research Assistance:** AI can quickly gather and summarize relevant information, providing valuable insights and data to support your narrative.
- **Editing and Proofreading:** AI-powered platforms can help refine language, ensure grammatical accuracy, and maintain a consistent tone throughout the manuscript.

Turning Your Expertise into a Published Book, Faster Than Ever

Let's talk about something we see all the time. So many entrepreneurs dream of writing their book, but life gets busy, and somehow it always ends up on the back burner. Sound familiar? That's where we come in. When we work with clients, we show them how to use AI tools to jumpstart the book-writing process and speed it up dramatically.

With the help of AI, what used to take a year or more can now be drafted, edited, and polished in just a few months. AI can help you build the outline, generate topics, and spark ideas, but your unique voice, experiences, and insights are still what make the book truly powerful.

You can also lean into our **10x10x3** formula, which we teach in our book *The Strategic Writing System*, to structure your content quickly and easily.

And the results? Publishing a book doesn't just check a box. It skyrockets your credibility. Our clients have landed major speaking engagements, expanded their consulting businesses, and become recognized authorities in their industries, all because they finally got their message out there.

We've seen this over and over again. We've published over 3000 books, and every single one of our authors has become a #1 bestseller. And if there's one thing we know for sure, it's this: publishing a book is more than just an accomplishment. It's a strategic asset that sets you apart, builds your brand, and unlocks doors you didn't even know were waiting for you.

Here's how we leverage AI to **streamline the book creation process:**

1. **Expertise Extraction:** Using AI to capture and organize your unique frameworks, methodologies, and insights.
2. **Content Development:** Transforming those ideas into cohesive, compelling chapters.
3. **Editing and Refinement:** Using AI tools to polish the language while maintaining your authentic voice.

4. **Marketing and Launch Strategy:** Creating AI-generated marketing materials that position your book for maximum impact.

The real magic happens when you use AI not just as a helper, but as a true partner, from the first idea all the way through to your book's launch. In today's world, it's not just about publishing a book; it's about publishing the *right* book that sets you apart as the go-to authority in your field.

What is the 10x10x3 Writing Formula?

The 10x10x3 formula is a simple but powerful system designed to help you write your book faster and with less overwhelm. Here's how it works: First, brainstorm the top 10 questions people always ask you about your business, expertise, or industry. These are the questions your audience is most curious about. Then, take the time to thoughtfully answer each one, either by writing them out or speaking them into a recorder or transcription app like Otter.ai. Each answer should be about 3 to 10 minutes long, which is roughly the perfect length for a chapter. Next, list the top 10 "should ask" questions, the ones people *don't* think to ask, but really should. These are the hidden gems that set you apart and reveal your deeper expertise. For each question or topic, add 1 to 3 personal, client, or relatable stories that illustrate your points and connect emotionally with your readers. When you follow this structure, you'll have a full, authentic manuscript that flows naturally, positions you as an authority, and feels easy and rewarding to create. It's the perfect framework to finally get your book out of your head and into the world!

What are FAQs?

FAQs are the questions you get asked over and over again about your business, product, or service. I hear it all the time, people saying, "You can't write a good book in just a few days or weeks." And I say, nonsense!

You're already writing your book every week when you answer the same questions for your clients. If you just captured those answers, packaged them into a book, a tool people trust and admire, you'd have a powerful marketing asset. Not only can it bring in new business, but it can get you media interviews, podcast appearances, speaking gigs, and more! When we turn these FAQs into book chapters, we also think smart: phrasing the questions with keywords people actually search for, like, "How do you write a great business book in the shortest amount of time?"

What are SAQs?

SAQs are the "Should Ask Questions", the ones people *should* be asking but don't. If they only knew what you knew they would ask you this. For example, if you were a realtor, instead of just asking me what's the best area to buy houses in, you should be asking me, what area has the best schools and appreciates the most. When you answer these smart questions, you're not just giving value, you're building trust and blowing people away with your expertise. It's like giving someone a shortcut that saves them years of trial and error. When you show up with that kind of insight, people realize you're the real deal, and they *want* to work with you. This is where the selling gets easy, because you've already earned their trust.

What is a Story?

A story is what makes your book come alive. It's a slice of real life, your experience, a client's journey, or even something you've heard that ties into your message. Stories make you relatable. They help your reader feel connected to you because they see themselves in your journey. And here's the secret: facts tell, but stories *sell.* They turn information into an experience your readers won't forget. So when you write your book, don't just tell people what you know, *show* them through powerful stories that invite them in and keep them turning the pages.

What is a Lesson?

The lesson is where you teach your expertise at a deeper level. It's different from just answering a question; it's where you solve their bigger problem and share the ah-ha moments that changed everything for you. This is where you shine as the authority. Your lessons guide your reader through what they didn't know they needed, and they walk away feeling smarter, stronger, and more connected to you.

VIP Book Creation Day: A Smarter Way to Write Your Book

Writing a book can feel overwhelming, especially when you're balancing a business, a career, and a busy life. That's why we developed the VIP Book Creation Day, an approach designed to help authors move from idea to organized, actionable content in just one focused day. Spend the day with a professional ghostwriter and business development and publishing expert, where we take you from confusion to a fully organized book framework with up to 10,000 words written and placed inside the chapters.

The process begins with finding clarity on your **"why"**, the deeper purpose behind your book, and what you want it to achieve. From there, we work together to uncover your unique voice, message, and stories so that the writing process feels more natural, enjoyable, and true to who you are. Before the VIP Day, you'll complete a thoughtful author assessment and join a Pre-Day call to set clear expectations and goals.

During the six-hour session, the focus is on creating real momentum. Together, we outline the structure of your book, define your main themes, identify your target audiences, and build an inventory of the content that needs to be created.

After the session, you'll receive a full transcript, a recording of the day's work, and a comprehensive document capturing your strategy, outline, and initial content. A follow-up call ensures you stay on track and feel supported as you continue the writing process.

The goal of the **VIP Book Creation Day** is simple: to make the journey of writing a book feel doable, inspiring, and strategic. When you have a clear plan and the right support, bringing your ideas to life becomes not only possible, but truly exciting.

Working with a Book Coach, Editor, and Ghostwriter

Writing a book is a big dream, and the truth is, you don't have to do it alone. In fact, you shouldn't! Having the right team around you makes all the difference.

A **book coach** is like having a personal trainer for your writing. They keep you focused, help you organize your ideas, and make sure you're moving forward with a clear plan. It's so much easier (and way more fun) when someone's guiding you step-by-step.

Then there's the **editor**, your secret weapon. Even the best writers need fresh eyes to make sure their message is crystal clear, their voice shines through, and everything flows beautifully. A great editor polishes your words so you can shine even brighter.

And if you're short on time or just not the "sit and type for hours" kind of person, the **ghostwriting process** might be perfect for you. A good ghostwriter takes your ideas, your stories, your voice, and brings it all together into a finished book that feels 100% like *you*.

At the end of the day, it's all about getting your message out into the world in a powerful, professional way. And when you have the right support, writing your book feels less like climbing a mountain and more like taking an exciting, unforgettable journey.

The Power of Sitting Down and Simply Writing

While there are so many new tools and strategies out there to help you create your book faster, let's not forget that sometimes, the most powerful method is just sitting down and writing the old-school way.

There's something magical about giving yourself the time and space to simply pour your thoughts onto the page without overthinking it. No fancy apps, no shortcuts, just you, your ideas, and a blank screen (or a notebook if you're feeling extra classic!). Writing the traditional way helps you connect deeply with your voice, your stories, and your message. It gives you room to process your thoughts, refine your ideas, and let inspiration flow naturally. Some of the best books ever written came from this simple, consistent habit of showing up and writing a little every day.

"The magic happens when you show up for your story, and trust that it will show up for you."

So if you love the feel of putting pen to paper, or fingers to keyboard, go for it! Whether you write one page a day or carve out bigger chunks of time each week, steady progress will always get you there.

Remember, there's no *wrong* way to write your book. The important thing is to keep moving forward and trust that your story is worth telling.

The Book as a Business Asset

Your book is so much more than just pages filled with ideas; it's one of the most powerful business assets you'll ever create. A book positions you as the expert, the go-to authority who literally "wrote the book" on your topic. It doesn't just build credibility; it opens doors to speaking gigs, consulting work, and premium offers that can transform your business. Plus, it attracts high-value clients who already trust your expertise before they even meet you. And the best part? One well-crafted book becomes the foundation for an entire content ecosystem, fueling your blogs, social media, videos, and presentations, and keeping your message alive and growing for years to come.

Your book is a powerful business asset that can:

1. **Establish You as the Obvious Choice:** In a crowded market, a book sets you apart as the expert who literally "wrote the book" on your topic.

2. **Generate Passive Income:** Beyond the direct revenue from book sales, a strategic book opens doors to speaking engagements, consulting opportunities, and premium offers.

3. **Attract High-Value Clients:** Clients who read your book come to you pre-sold on your expertise and methodology, shortening the sales cycle and increasing conversion rates.

4. **Create a Content Ecosystem:** One book can be repurposed into countless pieces of content, blogs, social media posts, videos, presentations, and more, extending your reach and impact.

Book as Business Catalyst

Unknown Expert	Write the Book	Generate Income	Attract Clients	Create Content	Recognized Authority
Unrecognized in the market	Establish expertise and authority	Open doors to new opportunities	Pre-sold clients seek your expertise	Repurpose book into various formats	Obvious choice in your field

Case Studies: Using Your Book In Your Business

One of our clients, Stephanie Chung, is a perfect example of how a book can completely transform your business and brand authority. When Stephanie first came to us, she was already an accomplished speaker with a strong reputation, but she wanted to elevate her platform even further and create a more lasting impact after each event.

After publishing her book, the momentum started. Her speaking fees increased simply because having a book positioned her as the definitive expert in her field. Meeting planners and organizations saw her not just as a speaker, but as someone who had literally *written the book* on *How to Lead People Who Are Not Like You*.

Even better, Stephanie started selling even more books every time she stepped on stage. Imagine that, not only getting paid to speak, but walking away with hundreds of additional book sales after each appearance. She even worked the book sales into her speaker fee. She had companies like McDonald's, ABC, and more asking her to speak. It created a powerful stream of passive revenue and, even more importantly, allowed her message to **live on with the audience** long after the event was over. Her book became a bridge for deeper client relationships, further consulting opportunities, and future speaking invitations.

Stephanie's story shows that a well-crafted book isn't just a nice-to-have; it's a business-building, authority-amplifying, revenue-generating machine. When done right, your book becomes one of the most valuable assets you can create for your brand.

Another one of our incredible clients, Joshua Evans, is a **shining example** of what can happen when you take your knowledge, package it into a book, and leverage it the right way. Joshua had a wealth of expertise and a real passion for helping organizations build stronger, more engaged workplace cultures. But he needed a way to stand out, to show companies he was the authority they needed to bring in.

We worked together to take his ideas, experiences, and frameworks and turn them into **a powerful, polished book**. That book instantly elevated Joshua's credibility and opened doors he had only dreamed about before. In a short time, he transitioned into a six-figure speaking career, commanding over $10,000 per keynote and landing corporate engagements almost every month.

His book became the **ultimate business card**, one that didn't just introduce him but positioned him as *the* expert in his field. Event organizers and companies weren't just hiring a speaker; they were hiring an author, a thought leader, and a trusted advisor. His book also gave him something tangible to leave behind at events, deepening his impact with audiences and creating a ripple effect of new opportunities.

Joshua's story is living proof that when you use your book strategically, it's not just about having something to sell, it's about building a brand, creating authority, and unlocking a whole new level of business growth.

Summary

Publishing a book remains one of the most powerful ways to build authority, accelerate your brand, and unlock new revenue streams. Thanks to AI tools like ChatGPT, Claude, and custom GPTs, the writing and publishing process is now faster, easier, and more accessible than ever. By using smart frameworks like the 10x10x3 system, entrepreneurs can turn their expertise into high-impact books that elevate credibility, attract premium clients, create passive income, and fuel a full content ecosystem. A book isn't just a project; it is a strategic business asset that builds your empire for years to come.

Action Steps

1. Brainstorm 10 FAQs and 10 SAQs about your business to create a foundational book outline.

2. Use AI tools to draft, edit, or expand your book content while preserving your authentic voice.

3. Identify three client stories or personal experiences to weave into your book to build an emotional connection.

4. Create a clear goal for your book: authority building, client attraction, speaking engagements, or revenue generation.

5. If needed, engage a book coach, editor, or ghostwriter to accelerate your process and elevate your final product.

6. Develop a plan to use your book as the cornerstone of a larger content strategy for blogs, videos, and social media.

CHAPTER 7

CONTENT DOMINATION ON AUTOPILOT

You don't have to be everywhere, just everywhere that matters.

–Gary Vaynerchuk

Imagine waking up on a Tuesday morning. You don't immediately reach for your phone with a jolt of anxiety, wondering, "What am I going to post today?" Instead, you pour a cup of coffee and glance at your notifications. A new, insightful blog post under your name just went live on your website. Your email newsletter, filled with valuable tips and written in your unique voice, was just sent to your growing list. On LinkedIn, a thoughtful discussion is already brewing in the comments of an article you "published" an hour ago. On Instagram and TikTok, several short, engaging video clips from your last podcast interview are making the rounds, complete with perfect captions.

Your brand is everywhere, on blogs, in podcasts, across social media, and it all happened without you lifting a single finger that morning. This isn't a far-off fantasy. This is the magic of content domination on autopilot.

In today's hyper-fast, attention-starved digital world, visibility isn't just an advantage; it's a prerequisite for survival. If you're not consistently present, you are, for all practical purposes, invisible. The challenge, of course, is that being consistently present has traditionally required a Herculean effort. It felt like a choice: either you spend all your time creating content, or you spend all your time running your actual business. But what if that choice was a false one?

By strategically planning your content, diversifying your formats, and leaning into the almost unbelievable power of modern AI tools, you can create, publish, and engage with more impact than a 10-person marketing team from just a few years ago. You can build a steady, vibrant, and authentic presence that captures attention, builds deep trust, and keeps your ideal audience coming back for more, almost effortlessly.

How AI Helped Land a Speaking Gig at the United Nations, and How You Can Use It to Dominate Content Creation Too

Let's talk about something really exciting! You know how sometimes an incredible opportunity pops up, and you have just a teeny tiny window to make it happen? Well, my friend Mike Koenigs had one of those moments, and thanks to the magic of AI, he turned it into a total home run.

Here's the story: Mike got the chance to speak at the United Nations. Yes, you heard me right, the United Nations! But there was a catch (isn't there always?). He had less than 48 hours to get everything ready, and just four hours to submit a polished speech and biography that followed the UN's super-specific guidelines. Yikes!

Now, most people would have panicked, but not Mike. Instead, he leaned on AI to save the day. He jumped into ChatGPT and said, "Hey, I'm Mike Koenigs. I'm speaking to a group of senators, policymakers, and global leaders about AI, and I need to focus on women's entrepreneurship and equal access to technology. Oh, and it needs to sound just right for the UN."

Within minutes, and I mean minutes, not hours or days, AI started asking smart, clarifying questions. Fifteen minutes later, Mike had a beautifully crafted, UN-approved biography ready to go. Then, to nail down the speech, Mike and his wife (who's a humanitarian rock star herself) did a quick brainstorm using Otter.ai to capture all their ideas. He popped that transcript into ChatGPT, and *boom*, a polished, professional, UN-style speech was born.

But Mike didn't stop there. Oh no. He used InVideo.ai to create a stunning visual presentation, imagine a dynamic video complete with B-roll footage, all to show how AI could break language barriers and connect people across the globe.

And guess what? Mike pulled it all off:

- Full speech and bio ready in less than an hour
- Nailed the official UN language without hiring a fancy consultant
- Delivered a jaw-dropping presentation that opened even more doors (yep, they invited him back!)

It's a real-life example of how AI isn't just a tool, it's your secret weapon to move faster, smarter, and bigger than you ever imagined.

Now, let me show you how you can turn your content machine on, keep it running, and have it work for you 24/7, while you sip your drink at the beach. Regular content creation is vital for maintaining visibility and engagement in today's digital landscape. A strategic approach involves:

- **Content Calendar:** Planning topics and publication dates in advance to ensure a steady flow of content.

- **Diverse Formats:** Utilizing blogs, videos, podcasts, and social media posts to cater to different audience preferences.

- **Audience Engagement:** Encouraging feedback and discussions to foster a community around your content.

Let's be real, keeping up with content creation can feel like a full-time job, right? But here's the exciting part: with AI in your corner, you can put so much of it on autopilot and still look like a total rockstar. AI tools can help you generate fresh ideas by suggesting trending topics based on what's buzzing in your industry, making sure your content stays timely and relevant. Need to whip up a blog post or a video script? No problem! AI can draft your first version in minutes, saving you hours of staring at a blank screen. Want to step up your game even more? Use AI-driven platforms to create videos, podcasts, and other multimedia content without needing a full production team. And here's one of my favorite hacks: have AI help you draft a full social media calendar. Start with a month's worth of posts. Once you see it's getting your style and voice right, challenge it to build out your social calendar for the whole quarter, or even the entire year! Talk about a game changer. With the right AI tools in place, you'll be creating, posting, and connecting like never before, and doing it all with way less stress.

Quick Checklist: How to Use AI for Effortless Content Creation

- **Generate Fresh Ideas:**
  Ask AI to suggest trending topics so your content is always current and relevant.

- **Draft Your Content Fast:**
  Use AI to create first drafts of blogs, articles, and video scripts; no more staring at a blank page!

- **Produce Multimedia Content:**

  Create videos, podcasts, and even B-roll footage with AI-driven platforms, without a big production team.

- **Build a Social Media Calendar:**

  Have AI draft a full month of social media posts.

  - Love what you see? Then let it map out your content for the entire quarter, or even the whole year!

- **Save Time and Stay Visible:**

  Let AI handle the heavy lifting so you can focus on shining your light and connecting with your audience!

The Modern Content Strategy: Calendar, Formats, and Community

Before we dive into the "how" of AI, we need to understand the "what" of a successful content strategy. AI is a powerful engine, but it needs a roadmap to follow.

The Content Calendar: Your North Star. A content calendar is your single source of truth. It's where you plan your topics, themes, and publication dates in advance. This simple act transforms you from a reactive content creator (panicked and posting on the fly) to a proactive strategist. You can plan for holidays, product launches, and industry events, ensuring a steady, reliable flow of high-value content that your audience learns to anticipate.

Diverse Formats: The Language of Your Audience. Not everyone consumes content in the same way. Some people love to read deep-dive blog posts. Others prefer to listen to a podcast during their commute. Many are visual learners who are captivated by video. A dominant content strategy caters to all of them, often by repurposing a single core idea into multiple formats. A Book or podcast episode becomes a blog post, which becomes a series of quote graphics, which becomes a short video clip.

Audience Engagement: From Monologue to Dialogue. The goal of content isn't just to broadcast; it's to connect. Great content encourages feedback, sparks discussions, and asks questions. It fosters a genuine community around your brand, making your audience feel seen, heard, and valued. This is how you build a tribe of loyal fans who not only buy from you but become your most vocal advocates.

The thought of managing all of this, a calendar, multiple formats, and constant engagement, is where most experts throw their hands up in despair. It feels like a full-time job. But this is precisely where AI changes the entire equation.

With AI in your corner, you can put the vast majority of this process on autopilot and still show up as an authentic, engaging rockstar. AI can generate endless, relevant ideas by analyzing trending topics in your niche. It can draft that.

Building Your Own Content Domination System While Reclaiming Your Time

Now, here's the part where I get super excited, because you can do this too. Yep, you don't have to be speaking at the United Nations to build your own content creation empire. You just need a system. Let's be honest, trying to keep up with content creation today can feel like a full-time job on top of your full-time job! But here's the good news: you don't have to do it all yourself anymore. With a smart system in place, and a little help from our AI friends, you can create more impact, stay totally authentic to who you are, and actually get your time back. Imagine that! So let's walk through it, step by step.

Document Your Core Expertise

You've got this amazing expertise inside of you, your story, your knowledge, your magic. But if you don't document it, how can you expect others to fully experience it? Think about it, consistency builds trust. It's not enough to just pop in with a post here and there. You want your voice, your vibe, your brilliance to show up everywhere you are, blog posts, emails, podcasts, videos, and feel completely *you*.

This is why the first step is to create a personal knowledge base, or what I call your "External Brain." This is a central repository of your core ideas. Use a tool like Google Docs, Notion, or Obsidian. Start documenting:

- Your Frameworks: What are the 3, 5, or 7 steps in your signature process?
- Your Core Stories: Your origin story, key client case studies, "aha" moments.
- Your FAQs: What questions do you answer over and over again?
- Your Best Content: Gather transcripts of your talks, your most popular articles, and your best social media posts.

Content Creation Strategy

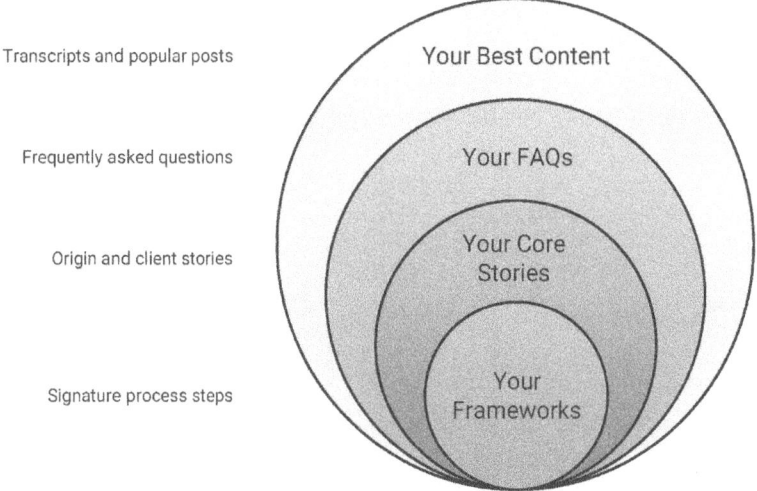

Once you have this raw material, I love using ChatGPT to create a personalized writing style guide. You can feed it your best content and prompt it: "Analyze the attached documents to create a detailed Brand Voice and Writing Style Guide. Identify my tone, vocabulary, sentence structure, use of analogies, and overall personality. Create a blueprint so that any future writing can replicate this style."

This style guide becomes the foundational document for all future AI-assisted content creation. It's how you clone your best self, allowing you to scale your content without ever feeling like you've sold out or lost your authentic voice.

Create Your Brand Voice and Customer Profile

Now, here's the next piece, and it's just as important. You have to know *exactly* **who you're talking to**. Not just kinda-sorta. Not "everyone who likes business books." No, you want your content to land so well that your dream client feels like you're reading their mind.

Using AI to help you carve out your Ideal Customer Profile (ICP) is a game-changer. It digs into your digital footprint and picks up on patterns you might not even realize. What are your people struggling with? What lights them up? What language do they use when they describe their problems? And can identify patterns you might have missed.

Prompt for ICP: "Analyze the attached client testimonials and social media comments. Create a detailed Ideal Customer Profile. Include their demographics, their biggest pain points and frustrations related to [Your Topic], their ultimate goals and aspirations, and the specific language they use to describe their problems."

When you know that, your content stops feeling generic and starts feeling magnetic. People will see your posts, your emails, your videos, and say, *"Oh my gosh, this is exactly what I needed!"* That's how you turn followers into fans, and fans into clients.

Deploy the Right Tools for Maximum Efficiency

Let's face it, sometimes it's not about working harder, it's about working smarter. And the right tools? They don't just save you time, they *unlock* creative opportunities you'd never have had otherwise. Let's talk about a few of my favorites:

- **Otter.ai** This one's like carrying a personal assistant in your pocket. Record ideas when you're walking, driving, or even while you're getting your morning coffee. Capture your genius in the moment, before it floats away.

- **CastMagic** Do you have a podcast? Great. Now turn it into blog posts, social posts, emails, a whole ecosystem of content from just one conversation.

- **OpusClip,** Do you have long videos just sitting there? Break them into bite-sized social clips with captions, perfect for grabbing attention on Instagram, LinkedIn, you name it.

- **Fyxer** Seriously, why are you still managing your inbox and calendar yourself? Let AI handle the admin grind so you can stay in your creative zone where you truly shine.

- **ChatHub** Imagine getting different perspectives from multiple AIs at once, it's like having your own little creative think tank!

Level Up with Advanced Production Tools

When you're ready to really start *owning* your space, these tools will take you there:

- **NotebookLM,** Create research-backed, citation-strong content that makes you look like the expert you are. Perfect for thought leadership pieces, articles, or your next big keynote.

- **Manus** and **GenSpark,** Got a podcast, webinar, or keynote talk? Don't just let it live and die there. Turn it into a full-fledged book or report. Yes, you can be a published author from content you've *already* created!

- **Lovable.dev**, Get a gorgeous, professional website or landing page up and running in days, not months. Because when inspiration strikes, you don't want to be waiting around.

Automate and Scale

Now, here's the magic sauce: automating and scaling.

When you connect your AI tools to your Google Drive, Gmail, Calendar, oh my gosh, it's like **finding buried treasure**. Old notes turn into new blog posts. Forgotten email drafts spark brand new marketing campaigns. It's all about taking what you already have and turning it into gold.

And here's one of my favorite strategies for content creation, the "10-80-10" rule. You put in the first 10%, the vision, the voice, the magic only *you* can bring. AI handles 80% of the heavy lifting, the drafting, structuring, and organizing. Then you come back for the final 10%, polishing and giving it your personal sparkle.

This way, you stay in control without getting bogged down. You stay the heart of your brand while your content engine keeps humming right along, spreading your message far and wide.

By putting this system into play, you stop being the bottleneck in your own business growth. You become the strategic director of your brand, guiding it, leading it, but **no longer stuck in the weeds** of daily content production.

And guess what happens next? Your visibility skyrockets. You start attracting new opportunities without chasing them. People start coming *to you* because your voice, your mission, and your message are out there consistently, authentically, and powerfully.

So if you're ready to step out of the grind and into your greatest impact, it's time to build your content engine. Let's go expand your influence, elevate your brand, and change the world with your message.

The AI Authority Engine Approach to Content

Now, let's be honest, you can have a bunch of shiny tools, but if they're not working together, it's like trying to build a house with a pile of bricks and no blueprint. That's why the real magic, the *real power*, comes from putting all these pieces together into a *cohesive, strategic system*. We call it the **AI Authority Engine**, and let me tell you, it changes the game. Here's how it works and why you're going to want us in your corner to build it for you:

First, we help you Extract Your Unique Expertise.

You're not just another voice online; you have a unique story, a powerful set of skills, frameworks, and ways you see the world that nobody else has. Our team works with you personally to pull all of that gold out of your head and heart, the stuff you might not even realize is your secret sauce, and frame it in a way that's powerful, clear, and magnetic to your audience. This isn't **cookie-cutter branding**. This is about showing the world what makes you **truly unforgettable**.

Next, we help you write the book or manifesto that defines your message and locks in your authority.

Your book isn't a vanity project; it's your positioning, your thought leadership, and your intellectual property in a format that scales trust. We guide you step-by-step through the process of extracting your framework, your stories, your philosophy, and your client wins and turn them into a compelling, publishable asset that becomes the cornerstone of your content empire. When your message is codified in a book, everything else becomes easier: content creation, PR, podcast interviews, client conversion. We don't just help you write it; we help you leverage it **like a pro**.

Then, we create a content multiplication system.

Here's the truth: in today's fast-paced world, you can't afford to create one blog post here, a podcast there, and a video six months later. You need a system that turns *one* brilliant idea into *ten* or even *twenty* pieces of high-impact content across multiple platforms, and we set that system up for you. It's about working smarter, not harder, and finally seeing your message everywhere without burning yourself out.

Then, we implement AI-powered workflows tailored just for you.

We're not just tossing you generic tools and saying "good luck!" Oh no. We actually build custom GPTs (AI assistants) that are trained specifically in your voice, your expertise, and your brand personality. That way, when content goes out, it sounds exactly like you, not like some robot wrote it. It's *your* voice, your style, your heart, just multiplied and streamlined.

And finally, we build a digital authority Infrastructure.

Because here's the thing, it's not just about creating content. It's about creating *smart* content. Strategic content. We make sure everything you put out into the world is positioned not only to attract and engage *real people* but also to make you more discoverable by the AI-driven algorithms that decide what gets seen, what gets shared, and who rises to the top. We're building your digital footprint in a way that works for you today *and* sets you up to win in the future.

So why work with us?

Because we don't just help you "do more", we help you *be more visible, be more trusted,* and *become the obvious choice* in your space. We know how to pull out your brilliance, wrap it in strategy, power it with AI, and position it so that your influence grows exponentially, without you having to hustle 24/7. If you're serious about scaling your authority, impact, and business growth, then the **AI Authority Engine** is the fastest, smartest, and most authentic way to do it. And we are here to help you build it.

To learn more about working one one-on-one with Jenn and Melanie and their team to be your Fractional AI Officer and create your **AI Authority Engine,** visit BeRecognized.us

Think Bigger, Not Harder:

Instead of asking, "What should I post today?" ask, "How can one piece of content become ten?" Start planning with a multiplication mindset.

This chapter shows you how to build a content machine that works 24/7 to grow your brand and your business, even when you're on vacation or deep in client work. It's about building your authentic voice into an AI-powered system that keeps showing up, so you don't have to manually post every single day. Let's stop thinking about what to post every day, and start thinking about how one idea can transform into ten powerful messages.

You're not just building content... you're building an empire. So let's get you out of obscurity and into omnipresence. Remember, your voice matters. Let's make sure the world hears it loud and clear, even while you're sleeping.

Reach Out to Our Team:

If you want the fastest, most strategic path to building your **AI Authority Engine,** without trial, error, and guesswork, **connect with us.** We'll help you put it all together, so you can rise faster, stay authentic, and turn your influence into real-world results.

Ready to work with us to build your content empire?

Is time more valuable than money to you? Let's chat. Apply now at BeRecognized.us and let's bring your vision to life.

Action Steps: Your First Week of Content Domination

Let's turn this knowledge into immediate momentum. Here's your plan for the next seven days:

1. Document Your Expertise (2 Hours): Start a "My Brain" Google Doc. Spend two hours outlining 3-5 of your core signature frameworks or methods. What are the key steps you always teach your clients?

2. Identify Your Voice (1 Hour): Copy and paste your 3 favorite articles or social media posts you've ever written into ChatGPT. Use the prompt from Step 1 above to create your V1 Brand Voice guide.

3. Define Your Audience (1 Hour): Use the ICP prompt from Step 2 to analyze your existing client data or testimonials. Get a clear, one-page summary of who you're talking to.

4. Set Up Two Core AI Tools (30 Mins): Sign up for Otter.ai and CastMagic (or a similar tool). Connect them to your accounts.

5. Run Your First "10-80-10" Test (1.5 Hours): Record a 15-minute audio file in Otter.ai talking about one of your core frameworks. Upload it to CastMagic. Take the assets it generates and spend 30-45 minutes polishing the blog post and a few social posts. Publish one. Feel the power.

6. Reach Out to Our Team: If you want the fastest, most strategic path to building your complete AI Authority Engine—without the guesswork—connect with us. We'll help you put it all together, so you can rise faster, stay authentic, and turn your influence into unimaginable results.

PART III

MONETIZING
YOUR EXPERTISE

CHAPTER 8

HIGH-TICKET OFFERS AND STRATEGIC POSITIONING

If you don't value your expertise, the market won't either.

–Melanie Johnson

Have you ever looked at someone and thought, "How are they charging *that much* for what they do?" Maybe even felt a tiny pang of, "Hey, I know just as much as they do!", but you're not quite there yet in your pricing or business model?

Trust me, you're not alone.

And guess what? It's not because they're smarter, better, or luckier. It's because they've strategically positioned themselves, packaged their brilliance the right way, and created high-ticket offers that people *can't wait* to pay for.

In this chapter, we're diving into how you can do exactly that.

Imagine creating offers that not only light you up but also command premium pricing, without feeling salesy or pushy. Offers that create real transformation for your clients, give you freedom and scalability, and truly honor the value of your work. Ready? Let's dig in.

Why High-Ticket Offers Are the Game Changer You've Been Waiting For

Here's the deal:

When you have a solid authority foundation (and if you've been following along, you're building that beautifully!), new doors start to swing wide open for you. Suddenly, monetizing your expertise becomes so much easier and way more exciting.

Some of the avenues that naturally open up include:

- **Consulting Services:** Offering personalized advice to companies that need your expertise but don't know where to start.
- **Online Courses:** Sharing your knowledge in a structured, scalable way for those eager to learn from you.
- **Speaking Engagements:** Getting paid (well!) to show up, share your wisdom, and build even more authority.

Here's a little secret:

The people who pay the most *implement the fastest, stay committed longer,* and get *better results.*

And who doesn't want that kind of dream client, right?

Creating High-Ticket Offers and Premium Programs

Let's make it real practical: what kinds of high-ticket offers can you create?

Here's a peek at what's working right now:

- **Exclusive Workshops:**

  Small, high-value sessions for select clients who want direct access to your strategies and insights. Think VIP days, masterclasses, or intensives.

- **Retainer Services:**

  Ongoing support, like having you on their "team" month after month, ensures consistent growth and results. Predictable income for you, incredible value for them.

- **Licensing Your Content:**

  Ever dreamed of your work reaching hundreds, even thousands, without you personally delivering it? Licensing your proprietary methods and materials lets other businesses use your systems while you earn passive income.

Question for you:

Which of these feels the most exciting right now? Which one would light you up to offer?

The Power of Strategic Offer Design

Now, here's the heart of it, and where the magic really happens.
It's not just *what* you offer that matters.
It's *how you position it* that changes everything.

Here's the formula for creating irresistible high-ticket offers:

1. Focus on Transformation, Not Information

People aren't paying for "stuff."
They're paying for a *new reality.*
They want to go from stressed to confident, lost to laser-focused, and stuck to successful.

Ask yourself:

Can you clearly describe the "before and after" journey you offer?
Can you paint a vivid picture of the transformation?

If not, that's your first assignment. Get crystal clear on that transformation.

2. Create a Unique Methodology

You know what makes you different? Your way of doing things.
Give your method a name. Brand it.
Structure your process into a framework, a roadmap, or a system.

People don't comparison shop when they see your unique method; they see YOU as the only option.

Example:

Instead of "business coaching," offer "The Freedom Accelerator Method: A 90-Day System to Build a Scalable, AI-Enhanced Business."

Doesn't that sound way more valuable?

3. Build Scarcity and Exclusivity

Let's be real, people want what they *can't easily get.*
If everyone can work with you anytime, the perceived value drops.

Create natural scarcity:

- Limited seats.
- Invitation-only access.
- Application-based programs.

Pro Tip:

Position yourself as the prize. You're not chasing clients, you're selecting partners to join your transformation journey.

4. Layer in High-Touch and High-Tech

The most scalable offers combine *human connection* with *smart automation.*

Think:

- Private coaching calls (high-touch)
- AI-driven resources, templates, assessments (high-tech)

It's the perfect blend. Clients feel personally supported, but you aren't trading all your hours for dollars.

Real-World Case Study: From Free Content to a Thriving Coaching Business

Let me tell you about an entrepreneur I worked with who totally rocked this.

They started by putting out free content on using AI in marketing, simple posts, quick videos, and occasional webinars. Nothing fancy.

At first, people soaked it up. But they weren't buying anything yet.

So what changed?

Strategic Offer Design.

Instead of offering everything to everyone, they built a *three-tiered suite* of offers:

- **Flagship Program ($25,000):** High-touch, 90-day AI business implementation for ready-to-scale entrepreneurs.
- **Group Coaching ($8,000):** Collaborative guided implementation, a little more DIY, but still with strong support.
- **Self-Paced Course ($2,000):** Full AI business setup training for those who prefer to work at their own speed.

Within the first year, they crossed six figures, *without launching a million different things.*

One message. One system. Three smart options.

AI-Enhanced Delivery Models: Making It Even Easier (and More Profitable)

You know I love giving you practical tools, right? Let's level this up even more.

Here's how AI makes your delivery even stronger and easier:

- **Custom GPTs for Client Support:**

  Imagine having an AI assistant trained in your proprietary system, available 24/7 to answer questions, deliver support, and keep your clients moving forward.

- **Personalized Implementation Plans:**

  Use AI to analyze a client's starting point and instantly generate a step-by-step custom roadmap. (Saves you hours of manual work!)

- **Ongoing Optimization:**

  Set up AI-driven feedback loops to track client progress and recommend tweaks over time, making your offer *even more valuable* the longer people stay.

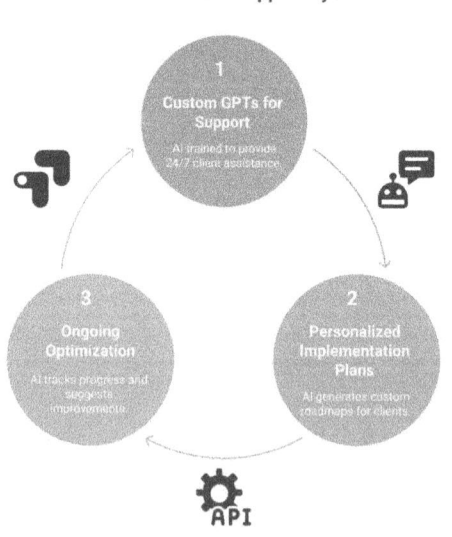

AI-Driven Client Support Cycle

This is how you scale results, not just sales. And *that* is how you create offers people rave about and refer others to.

Final Thoughts: Building a Business You Love, and Clients are Thrilled to Pay For

You're not here to hustle for low-ticket sales.

You're here to build a brand, an empire, a movement that honors the value of what you know and transforms lives along the way.

High-ticket offers, designed the right way, allow you to:

- Create a deeper impact for fewer, more committed clients
- Reclaim your time and energy
- Grow your income (and your freedom) exponentially
- Feel proud of the work you're putting into the world

But you don't have to do it alone.

This is what we do best.

At Elite Online Publishing's **AI Authority Engine**, we specialize in helping entrepreneurs, coaches, and experts like you *package your genius, position yourself like the authority you are,* and *build high-ticket offers that feel natural, aligned, and wildly profitable.*

SUMMARY

Let's be real, if you're not positioning yourself as a premium expert, you're probably leaving money and impact on the table. In this chapter, we uncovered the mindset and mechanics behind building irresistible high-ticket offers that not only elevate your income but also amplify your authority and freedom.

You learned how high-ticket offers, like exclusive workshops, retainer services, and licensed content, can open the door to your dream clients. Those who take action, stay longer, and get better results.

But the secret sauce? It's in how you design and position your offers. Transformation sells, not just information. Brand your method, build in exclusivity, blend high-touch with high-tech, and use AI to streamline and scale.

Bottom line: You deserve to charge more, and serve better, all while doing what lights you up.

Action Steps

1. Define the Transformation

   Write out the "before and after" journey your clients experience, making it vivid, emotional, and results-driven.

2. Name Your Method

   Give your unique process a name, bonus points if it sounds exciting and outcome-focused. Structure it into steps, phases, or pillars.

3. Pick Your Offer Style

   Choose one: VIP Day, Retainer, Licensing, Online Course, or Group Program. Which one energizes you the most right now?

4. Add Exclusivity

   Decide how you'll limit access, like application only, limited seats, or invite-only. Create urgency with deadlines or seasonal enrollment.

5. Blend High-Touch and High-Tech

   Outline how you'll support clients personally, through calls or feedback, and decide what you can automate, like templates, AI tools, or check-ins.

6. Leverage AI Tools

   Create a GPT or chatbot to assist your clients with FAQ-style support. Use AI to personalize onboarding or roadmap delivery.

7. Position Yourself as the Prize

Update your branding, bio, and messaging to reflect your high-ticket status. Show up with confidence; your dream clients are waiting.

Ready for Your Next Step?

If you're ready to stop undercharging, stop spinning your wheels, and finally step into your high-ticket authority, let's talk!

Schedule a call with our team today, and let's design the premium business model your expertise deserves.

BeRecognized.us

We can't wait to help you shine even brighter.

CHAPTER 9

THE PERSONAL MONOPOLY: HOW TO OWN YOUR CATEGORY IN THE AGE OF AI

You don't need to be the loudest in the room. You need to own the conversation everyone wants to have.

–Melanie Johnson

Have you ever felt that frustrating, sinking feeling in the pit of your stomach? The feeling that comes from pouring your heart, soul, and countless hours into your business, only to feel like you're **screaming into a void**. You're on a hamster wheel, running twice as fast as everyone else, yet you end each day in the exact same spot. You find yourself constantly explaining your value, endlessly justifying your prices to skeptical prospects, and trying to shout over the deafening, cacophonous noise of a marketplace saturated with look-alikes, sound-alikes, and think-alikes.

You know you're good at what you do. You have the expertise, the experience, and the **genuine desire** to make an impact. But you're a best-kept secret, and frankly, you're exhausted from being the one keeping it. This isn't just a business challenge; it's an energy drain that seeps into every corner of your life, making you question your path, your worth, and your sanity.

If this resonates, I want you to hear this **loud and clear:** This is not a business problem. It is not a marketing problem. It is a fundamental positioning problem.

And here is the urgent, **uncomfortable truth** of our time: Artificial Intelligence is not the magic bullet you've been hoping for. For the entrepreneur who is already lost in the sea of sameness, AI is not a life raft. It is a tidal wave. It is a powerful accelerant poured onto a fire that's already burning your business to the ground.

Think about it. When every single one of your competitors has access to the same generative AI tools, the same content templates, the same automated social media schedulers, and the same strategic outlines, the game fundamentally changes. The barrier to entry for creating more noise has just dropped to zero. The ability to produce an endless stream of mediocre, generic, "good enough" content is now a universal commodity. The winners in this new era are not those who can produce the most, the fastest. The winners are not the loudest. The winners are those who generate the most signal. They are the ones who are positioned **so uniquely, so authentically, and so authoritatively** that they have virtually no competition.

This is why building your Personal Monopoly is no longer a "nice-to-have" marketing strategy. It is the single most critical strategic asset you can create. It is your only sustainable advantage in the age of AI. Once you understand this and lock it in, the entire dynamic of your business shifts. You stop competing. You start creating. You stop chasing. You start attracting. You stop being a commodity and start becoming a category.

What Is a Personal Monopoly (and Why It's Your Only Sustainable Advantage)?

A Personal Monopoly is not about market domination in the traditional, ruthless, Rockefeller sense of the word. It's not about crushing your competitors or putting everyone else out of business. It is about architecting a market space so unique to you that you are the only occupant. It's about creating a category of one.

It is that inimitable, uncopyable, and wholly authentic fusion of your core components, all woven together into an unforgettable package. Let's break those components down:

- Your Specific Expertise: This is the "what you do." It's your skill, your craft, honed over years of practice and experience. But it's not just the general skill; it's the specific application of that skill to a particular problem.

- Your Hard-Won Perspective: This is the "how you see it." It's your unique worldview, your philosophy, your opinions, and your beliefs about your industry and your clients' problems. It's what you stand for and, just as importantly, what you stand against.

- Your Personal Story: This is the "why you do it." It's the narrative of your journey, including the struggles, the failures, the "aha" moments, and the ultimate triumphs that led you to this place of expertise. Your story builds connection and trust in a way that a resume never can.

- Your Unique Delivery Style: This is the "how you show up." Are you a fiery motivator, a calm and methodical teacher, a data-driven analyst, or a witty entertainer? Your style is the personality of your brand, and it attracts a specific type of client who resonates with your energy.

- Your Core Values: These are the non-negotiable principles that guide your work and life. They are the bedrock of your brand, influencing who you work with, what projects you take on, and how you conduct yourself.

Building a Unique Brand Identity

A Personal Monopoly weaves all five of these elements together. It's what makes you the only logical, emotional, and rational choice for a very specific client, who is facing a very specific problem, and who deeply resonates with your very specific way of solving it. It is the art of becoming irreplaceable in a world of endless replacements.

Let's paint a few pictures to make this tangible:

- Before: You're a "therapist." You are one of hundreds of thousands, competing on insurance panels and locations.

- After: You are "the go-to therapist for tech founders dealing with the psychological stress of a co-founder breakup." You have a waiting list, charge premium private-pay rates, and get invited to speak at tech conferences.

- Before: You're a "graphic designer." You bid for projects on freelance platforms, constantly justifying your hourly rate.

- After: You are "the brand identity specialist for ethical and sustainable CPG brands who want their packaging to tell a story." You work on retainer with high-growth companies that value your specific expertise.

When you achieve this level of positioning, the entire psychological dynamic shifts, both for you and your clients. For you, the frantic, needy energy of **"please pick me"** is replaced by the calm, grounded confidence of **"I am here for those who are ready."** Imposter syndrome dissolves because you are no longer trying to be a better version of someone else; you are simply operating as the truest version of yourself. For your clients, their feeling of being overwhelmed and confused is replaced by the profound relief of clarity. They feel seen, understood, and certain that they have finally found the answer they've been searching for.

So, I'll ask you again: What is the mental real estate you own in your market's mind? When they think of [the problem you solve], does your name, your face, your brand immediately come to mind? Or are you still a whisper in a hurricane of digital noise? It's okay if the answer is no. Recognizing this gap is the first, most crucial step toward building something truly remarkable. That's why we're here.

The Monopoly Triangle: Your Architectural Blueprint for Market Ownership

To build this fortress of authority, you need three pillars working in perfect, synergistic harmony. I call it the Monopoly Triangle. It is a self-reinforcing system. Neglect one side, and the entire structure becomes wobbly and vulnerable. But build all three, and you create an unshakeable foundation for your brand.

Be Known for One Thing (The Pillar of Hyper-Specificity)

The fastest path to obscurity is to be a generalist. In your desire to help everyone, you end up resonating with no one. The old saying, "the riches are in the niches," is more relevant today than ever. But we must update it for the AI age: The authority, the influence, and the income are in the ultra-specificity.

You must pick a clear, tangible, and deeply transformational outcome that you can deliver better than anyone else on the planet. The more laser-focused you are, the less competition you face, the more you can command premium fees, and the easier it is to become the recognized leader.

- Instead of: "I help people with their finances."
- Try: "I help ER doctors in their 40s create a tax-efficient real estate portfolio to enable early retirement."

The Fear of Niching Down: Why It's Holding You Back

Right now, you might be feeling a sense of panic. "But if I get that specific, I'll be turning away so much potential business! I'll lose out on clients!" This is the single most common fear that keeps brilliant experts trapped in the prison of being a commodity. It is also completely wrong.

Being a generalist means you are competing with millions. Being a specialist means you are competing with a handful. When you are hyper-specific, you don't lose clients; you repel the wrong clients, the ones who drain your energy, haggle on price, and don't value your true genius. Simultaneously, you become an **irresistible magnet** for the right clients. These are the people who have been searching desperately for someone who understands their unique context. When they find you, price becomes a secondary concern; the primary concern is securing a spot to work with you. You trade a large volume of low-quality leads for a steady stream of high-quality, pre-sold clients.

Your Action Step: What is the one, undeniable transformation you are willing to plant your flag on and commit to owning for the next three years? Write it down. Make it painfully specific. If it doesn't make you slightly nervous, it's not specific enough.

Build Undeniable Proof (The Pillar of Demonstrable Authority)

You cannot simply anoint yourself an expert. Authority in the digital age must be demonstrated and discoverable. If someone can't find proof of your expertise through a simple Google search, then for all practical purposes, your expertise doesn't exist. Your digital footprint is your new resume.

This means meticulously creating a body of work that acts as your silent salesperson, working 24/7 to build trust and credibility on your behalf. This isn't just about a few good testimonials. It's about building layers of proof, creating a powerful mosaic of authority.

Owned Authority vs. Borrowed Authority: You need both. Owned Authority is the content and intellectual property you create and control, your book, your proprietary framework, your blog, your podcast. This is your home base. Borrowed Authority is when another trusted entity lends you their platform and credibility, such as being interviewed on a major podcast, writing for a respected industry publication, or speaking at a well-known conference. A robust authority strategy leverages both.

What a Powerful Case Study Really Is: It's not just "Client X got great results." It's a compelling story that follows a clear narrative:

1. **The Problem:** Detail the specific, painful situation the client was in before they met you.

2. **The Process:** Explain how you applied your unique framework or methodology to their problem.

3. **The Results:** Showcase the tangible, measurable "after" state. Use numbers and metrics whenever possible.

4. **The Testimonial:** A direct quote from the client that adds emotional resonance to the data.

The Power of a Book: Publishing a book remains the gold standard of authority. But it must be the right book. It shouldn't be a simple regurgitation of common knowledge. A truly powerful book introduces a new idea, a new perspective, or a proprietary framework that changes the way the reader thinks about their problem. It is your manifesto.

Your Action Step: Conduct an "authority audit." Google yourself right now. What does the first page of results say about you? Is it a mountain of undeniable proof, or a molehill of vague claims? List three specific pieces of authority: one book chapter outline, one detailed case study, and one pitch to a podcast that you will create in the next 90 days.

Be Uncopyable (The Pillar of Personal Identity)

This is the deep, wide moat around your castle. It's what makes you defensible in a world where everything can be copied. Your service offerings can be copied. Your course curriculum can be duplicated. Your marketing templates can be stolen overnight.

But you, your story, your voice, your unique combination of experiences, cannot be replicated. This is your ultimate, sustainable, competitive advantage.

Name and Trademark Your Brilliance: Stop calling your work "coaching" or "consulting." Package your process, your methodology, your unique system for getting results, and give it a name. The "5P Magnetic Messaging Method." The "7-Figure Legacy Framework™." The "Resilient Leader Protocol." Naming your IP turns an intangible service into a tangible asset. It creates curiosity and makes your work sound more valuable and proprietary.

Find and Master Your Voice: Your voice is the consistent personality that shines through your writing, your videos, and your speaking. It's the difference between content that informs and content that connects. How do you find it? Ask yourself: How would I explain my core concept to a brilliant but skeptical CEO? Now, how would I explain that same concept to my curious 10-year-old niece? Your true voice lies somewhere in the blend of that authority and that simplicity.

Weave Your Core Stories: People don't buy what you do; they buy why you do it. Your stories are the emotional glue that binds clients to your brand. You should have three core stories in your arsenal:

1. **Your Origin Story:** Why do you care so deeply about this work? What personal struggle or triumph led you here?
2. **The "Aha! Moment" Story:** When did you discover the core insight or framework that you now teach?
3. **The Client Transformation Story:** A compelling narrative of how you guided a client from pain to possibility.

Your Action Step: What is the unique fingerprint you leave on everything you create? What is your origin story? Take 15 minutes and write it down, unedited. What is one unique name you can give to your primary process or framework?

The 1-2-3 Framework for Activating Your Personal Monopoly

Now let's get tactical. Here is a simple, step-by-step framework to take these concepts from abstract ideas to concrete actions.

1. Industry Focus: Plant Your Flag and Conquer the Territory

Choose one industry, one audience, one type of client. Plant your flag and make a conscious decision to dominate the conversation in that specific sandbox. The temptation to be a generalist is the siren song of mediocrity. It leads to diluted messaging, feast-or-famine client cycles, and a constant, exhausting struggle for relevance. Specialists are sought out; generalists wait for referrals.

- How to Validate Your Chosen Industry:
  - ○ Market Viability: Is the market growing, shrinking, or stagnant? Use tools like Google Trends and industry reports to assess its health.
  - ○ Problem Urgency: Do the people in this market have a "bleeding neck" problem? Is the problem you solve an urgent, expensive, high-stakes issue for them, or a minor annoyance?
  - ○ Accessibility: Can you actually reach these people? Are there established podcasts, publications, LinkedIn groups, conferences, or associations where your ideal clients congregate? If you can't find where they gather, you can't market to them.

2. Signature Offers: Engineer the Client Journey

You do not need a confusing, overwhelming menu of 20 different services. You need a simple, elegant, and highly profitable offer suite that acts as a clear and compelling pathway for your perfect-fit clients.

- The Front-Door Offer (Trust Builder): A low-risk, high-value way for clients to experience your genius. This could be a paid diagnostic, a strategic audit, a small workshop, or your book. The goal is to prove your value and build trust, making the next step a logical conclusion. Price point: 200–2,000.

- The Core Offer (Transformation Engine): This is your flagship program or service. It's where you deliver the primary transformation you promised in your positioning. This should be a high-ticket offer, reflecting the significant value you provide. Examples: a 90-day accelerator, a done-for-you implementation service, a 6-month mastermind. Price point: 5,000–50,000+.

- The Continuity Offer (Long-Term Value): For your best clients who have completed the Core Offer and want to continue working with you. This creates predictable, recurring revenue and deepens your relationship with your biggest fans. Examples: a high-level mastermind, a monthly retainer for strategic advice, an alumni community.

3. Amplification Channels: Master Your Megaphone System

A brilliant message heard by no one changes nothing. You must be as strategic about amplification as you are about creation. Choose a maximum of three primary channels and commit to mastering them. Chasing every shiny new platform is a recipe for burnout and mediocre results. Deep beats wide.

- **Choosing Your Channels Strategically:** Don't just pick the channels you like; pick the channels where your ideal clients live. If you serve C-suite executives, mastering LinkedIn and getting on industry podcasts is non-negotiable. If you serve visual artists, Instagram and Pinterest are your battlegrounds.
- **The Three-Channel Synergy:** Your channels should work together as a system.

  1. Your Pillar Content Channel (e.g., Podcast/YouTube): This is where you publish your weekly, long-form, authority-building content.

  2. Your Social Engagement Channel (e.g., LinkedIn/Twitter): This is where you break down your pillar content into daily insights, engage in conversations, and build community.

3. Your Networking & Outreach Channel (e.g., Guest Podcasting/Strategic Partnerships): This is how you introduce your message to new, relevant audiences and build relationships with key players in your space.

How AI Multiplies Your Personal Monopoly (Not Replaces It)

Let's be unequivocally clear: AI does not create your unique perspective. It does not invent your proprietary framework from scratch. It has not lived your story. AI is a tool, a phenomenally powerful, world-changing tool, but it is a multiplier, not a creator. It is an amplifier for the voice that you already have. If your voice is **unique, powerful, and specific,** AI will make it heard around the world. If your voice is generic, timid, and soulless, AI will simply help you produce generic, soulless content at a scale that will make you more invisible than ever before.

But once your Personal Monopoly is established, once your positioning is sharp, your proof is built, and your identity is clear, AI becomes your secret weapon, your unfair advantage.

The Content Repurposing Engine: You record one 30-minute podcast episode explaining a key concept from your signature framework. You then feed the transcript to an AI with a specific prompt: "Act as my personal brand's content strategist. Your voice should be [describe your voice: e.g., 'authoritative, insightful, and slightly witty']. Based on the provided podcast transcript, generate the following assets: 1. A 1200-word, SEO-optimized blog post with a compelling title. 2.. Five thought-provoking LinkedIn posts, each from a different angle of the core topic, ending with a question. 3.Ten quote-based tweets. 4. A 3-part email mini-series to send to my newsletter, designed to teach the core concept and lead to a call-to-action for my 'Front-Door Offer'." In one hour, you have a week's worth of cohesive, on-brand content.

The Market Intelligence Analyst: AI can be your personal research assistant. Use it to analyze the broader market and refine your unique position. Prompt: "Analyze the top 10 articles and YouTube videos for the search term '[Your Broader Topic]'. Identify the common themes, the dominant perspectives, and most importantly, identify the 'content gaps', what important nuances or perspectives are being missed? Also, analyze forums like Reddit and Quora for this topic to understand the exact language and questions the target audience is using." This allows you to create content that is not only different but deeply resonant.

Case Study: Clark East – The Power of a Monopoly-First Approach

One of my favorite transformation stories is about Clark East, a lifelong entrepreneur with a wealth of experience. When Clark came to us, he wasn't a beginner. He had a lifetime of success. But after the 2009 real estate crash, he found himself in a new world, needing to re-establish his credibility. What he needed **was a brand** that matched the depth of his journey.

We didn't start with AI tools. We started with the Monopoly Triangle.

1. **Lock in the Monopoly:** We guided Clark to identify his "uncopyable" angle. He wasn't just another business success story. His true power was in his story of navigating immense adversity. His Personal Monopoly became: "the mentor for entrepreneurs navigating life's inevitable, unexpected interruptions." It was authentic, powerful, and 100% his.

2. **Build the Proof:** We helped him codify his wisdom into his fantastic book, "Life is a Series of Unexpected Interruptions." This tangible asset became the cornerstone of his authority, his irrefutable proof.

3. **Amplify with AI:** Only then, with his monopoly defined and his proof established, did we unleash the power of AI. We took

the core ideas from his book and his decades of experience and used AI as a multiplier. We created an engine that repurposed his unique perspective into consistent, high-value daily content reflecting his voice and values.

The results were a testament to the power of this sequence. Clark's visibility exploded. He wasn't just another voice; he was the voice of entrepreneurial resilience. He attracted a new wave of high-level clients who resonated deeply with his story. Today, Clark East isn't just known for his past business success; he is recognized as an icon of resilience and reinvention. The key wasn't AI. The key was his Personal Monopoly. The AI was just the megaphone.

SUMMARY

The most dangerous, precarious, and exhausting place in business today is not being unknown; **it's being amazing but utterly forgettable.** It's being a ship in the storm, tossed around by the waves of market trends and technological shifts, indistinguishable from the thousand other ships around you.

A Personal Monopoly transforms you from one of the ships into the lighthouse. You are steadfast, anchored, and a beacon of clarity. The right ships (your ideal clients) are not tossed around by the storm; they navigate directly toward your light.

You do not need to be the loudest. You do not need to work the hardest. You need to own the one singular idea, the one unique perspective, the one profound transformation that your audience is desperately searching for. When you do that, you exit the brutal, soul-crushing race to the bottom. You stop competing on price because your value is, by definition, incomparable. You stop chasing clients because your clarity and authority draw them to you. **You become the category leader** because you are the category.

The age of AI is here, and it presents a stark choice. You can use it to become a more efficient producer of generic noise, further entrenching yourself as a commodity. Or, you can do the essential human work first. You can build your Personal Monopoly, clarify your unique signal, and then use AI as the most powerful amplifier the world has ever known to **scale your impact, your income, and your legacy.**

The choice is yours. Are you ready to build?

Action Steps:

1. Pick Your One Thing

What's the specific result or transformation you want to be known for? Write it down. Make it so clear and focused that it sets you apart from everyone else. 2. Name Your Framework

Take your unique way of working—the method, process, or approach you use—and give it a name. This turns your service into a brand.

3. Tell Your Origin Story

Write a short version of why you do what you do. This should come from the heart. Your story is what builds trust and makes your brand unforgettable.

4. Audit Your Digital Footprint

Google yourself. What do people find? Make a list of three ways you can boost your online authority—like publishing a case study, appearing on a podcast, or sharing part of your framework in a blog post.

5. Choose Where to Be Seen

Pick three channels to share your message. One for deep content (like a blog or podcast), one for daily engagement (like LinkedIn), and one to get discovered by new people (like guest interviews or collaborations).

CHAPTER 10

SCALING YOUR BUSINESS WITH AI-DRIVEN SYSTEMS

If you're still trying to scale by working harder, you're already losing to the ones who are working smarter.

—Jenn Foster

Alright, let's get real for a second.

When you think about scaling your business, really growing it into the powerhouse you dream about, what's the first thing you picture?

More employees? A bigger office? Longer hours? More pressure?

Listen, that's the old way of thinking.

Growth and scaling are not the same.

You can "grow" yourself straight into exhaustion if you're not careful, bigger business, bigger headaches, less freedom.

True scale means multiplying your income, your impact, and your freedom, **without** multiplying your workload, stress, or payroll. And the fastest way to get there today?

You guessed it: **AI.**

I'm going to show you how to scale smarter, using AI-driven systems that free you up to live the life and run the business you actually want.

True Scale with AI

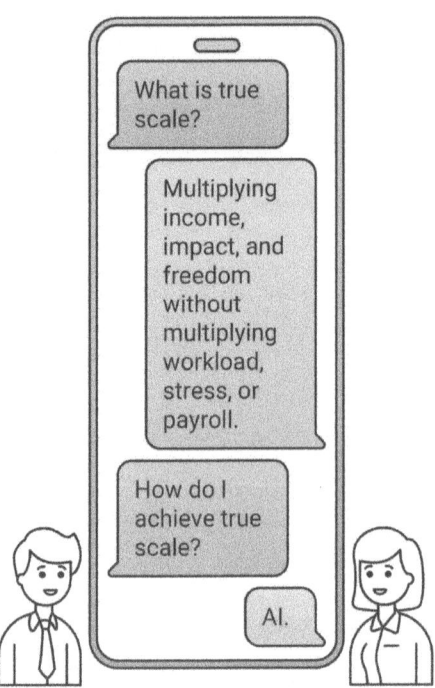

The Power of Automation: Where Real Scale Begins

You might be thinking, "Automation? Why should I even care? I'm busy enough already!" Automation is the difference between being a business owner and being your own overworked employee. And that's *exactly* why you *should* care. Here's the deal: if you don't automate, you're not really running a business, you're running yourself into the ground. You're the employee, the boss, the janitor, the receptionist, all rolled into one. Exhausting, right?

Now imagine this: what if you could hand off a bunch of that busy work? Free up hours in your day? Actually have time to think big, create new ideas, and yes, even kick back and *enjoy* the success you're building? (Crazy thought, I know.)

That's what automation does for you. It's not just a fancy tech word; it's your ticket to scaling your business without scaling your stress.

And here's the really exciting part:

With AI today, this kind of automation isn't just for giant corporations anymore. It's accessible, it's powerful, and honestly? It's essential if you want to compete.

Here's where you can jump in and make magic happen:

Lead Generation:

AI can find and qualify leads faster than any human team ever could, and it even spots those little "I'm ready to buy" signals that most of us would totally miss. Translation: more customers, less hustle.

Email Campaigns:

Imagine sending the perfect email, at the perfect time, to the perfect person, without even thinking about it. AI personalizes your messages, follows up like a champ, and keeps your audience engaged… while you're sipping your coffee or crushing your next big project.

Sales Processes:

Instead of answering the same basic questions over and over (and over) again, AI-powered chatbots and virtual assistants step in. They handle all that front-end stuff, so *you* can step into your genius zone, closing deals, building relationships, and making an impact.

So here's the million-dollar question I want you to really sit with:

Where are you still stuck doing work that AI could be doing faster, better, and cheaper for you?

Because friend, every minute you're spending on the wrong tasks is a minute you're stealing from your own success.

And you? You deserve more than just "busy." You deserve a breakthrough.

Building Scalable Systems for Client Acquisition

If you're serious about scaling, you can't build a business that depends on you being everywhere at once.

You Need Smart Systems. Period.

Here's How We Set It All Up:

Let's be real, if you're still trying to run your business off sticky notes and memory? You're *working way too hard* for way too little return. You need smart systems that think for you, work for you, and free you up to be the visionary you're meant to be.

Here's exactly what that looks like:

CRM Integration:

(That's Customer Relationship Management if you're wondering.)

An AI-powered CRM isn't just a fancy contact list. It's like having a crystal ball for your business. It doesn't just *store* your leads and customers, it *studies* them.

It watches their behavior, notices when they open your emails, tracks what they click on, and even predicts who's ready to buy, and *when* you should reach out.

Why you need it:

Because following up at the wrong time means you lose the sale.

Following up at the *right* time? That's when the magic happens.

With smart CRM integration, you're not guessing anymore. You're getting a tap on the shoulder that says, "Hey, call Sarah now. She's ready." And boom, another deal closed, another win.

Analytics and Reporting:

(Or, as I like to call it, your business's "health check-up.")

Look, if you're not tracking what's working and what's not, you're flying blind.

You wouldn't drive cross-country without a GPS, right?

Same thing here.

AI-driven reporting doesn't just throw numbers at you; it shows you real patterns, real trends. It tells you what products your customers love, where your sales are heating up, and where a little fire might be starting *before* it turns into a five-alarm disaster.

Why you need it:

Because if you can't measure it, you can't fix it.

Smart reporting lets you tweak and optimize every single part of your business, from marketing to sales to customer service, so you grow faster, smoother, and smarter.

Feedback Loops:

(Yes, feedback, but on autopilot!)

Normally, getting customer feedback can be slow, awkward, and sometimes downright painful.

But with AI, feedback becomes your *secret weapon.*

AI systems can automatically gather feedback after a sale, after a customer service call, after anything. Then it *analyzes* that data for you, finding trends you might not even see. Like maybe 20% of your customers are confused about your onboarding process. You didn't realize it, but now you do. So you can fix it *before* it costs you future sales.

Why you need it:

Because businesses that listen and adapt are the ones that win.

Every piece of feedback is a golden opportunity to get better, serve better, and grow faster, and smart systems make sure you never miss those chances.

Bottom Line:

If you want your business to scale, you've got to stop duct-taping it together.

Smart systems let you automate the stuff that bogs you down, so you can focus on the stuff that lifts you up, creating, leading, and making a real impact.

Because you deserve to work smarter, not harder.

The goal is simple:

> **Build a client acquisition machine that works whether you're in the office or on the beach.**

Growth vs. Scale: Why It Matters

Most entrepreneurs get trapped chasing "growth."

They think if they just hustle harder, everything will get better.

Wrong.

- **Growth** = more time, more people, more stress.
- **Scale** = more results, less chaos.

And AI?

AI is your fast-track to true scale, the kind that builds wealth, impact, and freedom, not just a longer to-do list.

Busy isn't the goal.

Freedom is.

Our Proven AI Business Scaling Framework

Let's get practical.

Here's the exact framework we use with our clients to create businesses that grow while their owners finally breathe again.

1. Document Your Core Processes

You can't automate what you haven't defined.

Get crystal clear:

- What tasks need your personal touch?
- What tasks are routine and ready for automation?

Map it all out, every step, every checklist.

2. Implement AI Automation

Once you've mapped it, automate it.

AI can easily take over:

- Scheduling
- Lead follow-up
- Initial client interactions
- Contracts and invoicing

Smart workflows mean your business runs like clockwork, whether you're there or not.

3. Develop AI Augmentation

Some things need your brilliance, but AI can still make them easier.

Use AI to:

- Draft emails, proposals, and reports
- Analyze feedback and data
- Suggest next steps based on real-time client behavior

Think of AI as your *high-performance teammate*, not your replacement.

4. Build AI-Powered Revenue Systems

Finally, make sure it all ties back to revenue.

- AI marketing funnels that nurture leads automatically
- Sales tools that move prospects through the pipeline
- Upsell and cross-sell systems that grow your client value, all while you're sleeping

This is how you scale revenue without scaling chaos.

Real-World Example: Building a Full Business in Just 3 Days with AI

Alright, let's talk real results.

You might be thinking, "Okay, Melanie, this AI stuff sounds cool, but does it really work in the real world?"

Oh, you bet it does, let me show you.

One of our clients came to us dreaming of launching a whole new brand. Normally, that's a huge mountain to climb, months of building a website, writing all the marketing material, planning a strategy, not to mention the crazy costs.

But guess what?

Using the right AI tools and smart workflows, we built **everything**,

- Full website
- Complete brand messaging
- Entire marketing strategy
- And even a first draft of a book

In just three days.

Not three months. Three days.

How?

- We used AI to create the brand story and messaging that connected emotionally with the audience.
- AI helped us draft and refine website content that would normally take a team of copywriters.
- We mapped out a full marketing plan, complete with email sequences, social media posts, and promotional ideas,   all powered by AI.

The result?

The client had a *fully operational business* ready to launch, faster, better, and at a fraction of the cost they were expecting.

Why should you care?

Because time is money, friend.

And when you can go from "idea" to "out in the world" in days instead of months, you're not just keeping up, you're leading.

That's the power of scaling smart with AI.

The Future-Proof Scaling Model

Here's the truth:

AI is moving fast. If you're not using it to scale now, you're already behind.

We teach a simple **Three-Horizon Model** for staying ahead:

- **Horizon 1 (Now):** Use today's AI tools to automate what's repetitive.
- **Horizon 2 (Next 12 Months):** Build custom AI solutions that fit *your* business.
- **Horizon 3 (Future):** Imagine brand-new business models that AI will make possible.

If you think big now, you'll dominate later.

Summary: Your Business Should Work FOR You

Scaling Your Business with AI-Driven Systems is a wake-up call for every entrepreneur still trying to hustle their way to the top. If you think scaling means longer hours, a bigger team, and more stress, oh honey, we need to talk. Real scale is about multiplying your income, your impact, and your freedom without multiplying your to-do list. And the golden key? It's AI. That's right, artificial intelligence is no longer just for the tech giants. You can use it right now to automate your lead gen, send the right email to the right person at the right time, and let chat-bots handle the questions you've answered a thousand times already. So while you're sipping your coffee or lounging at the beach, yes really, your business can still be working for you.

Now let's get practical, because you know I love a good system. First, you've got to map out your business processes—what needs your personal sparkle and what can be handed off. Then plug in AI to take care of all that repetitive stuff like scheduling, invoicing, follow-ups, and even drafting emails or reports. AI becomes your dream team. Add in a smart CRM that taps you on the shoulder and says, "Hey, call Sarah, she's ready to buy," and you're closing deals like a pro. We've had clients build entire brands, website, marketing plan, and even a book draft, in just three days. Three. Not months. Days. It's all about using the right tools in the right way. And listen, the future is coming fast. So whether you're just getting started or ready to build your next empire, scaling with AI isn't just smart, it's essential. Let's stop grinding and start scaling. You deserve to build a business that works for you.

Action Steps: Your Scaling Playbook

1. **Map Your Processes:**

   List everything you do that's repeatable. Identify what can be automated.

2. **Pick One Area to Automate:**

   Start small. Create a quick win. Build momentum.

3. **Implement a CRM:**

   If you don't have an AI-driven CRM yet, this is your first move. We can do this for you.

4. **Use AI to Augment Your Work:**

   Let AI draft your next email or client report, and watch your time savings add up.

5. **Think Bigger:**

   Where do you want to be in 12 months? Start setting up the systems now to get there.

Ready to scale smarter, not harder?

Let's build a business that works for *you*.

Schedule a call with our team today. Your next level is waiting.

BeRecognized.us

PART IV

FUTURE-PROOFING
YOUR BUSINESS

CHAPTER 11

THE AI REINVENTION MAP

Success in the future is not about predicting it. It's about preparing for a range of possibilities.

Paul Saffo

L et's have some real talk here.

If you're like most business owners right now, you've probably asked yourself at least once (or 100 times), "Where in the world do I even start with AI?"

And hey, I get it.

The buzz, the headlines, the new tools popping up every five minutes —it can all feel *completely overwhelming*.

But here's the truth no one's telling you:

You don't have to start perfect. You just have to start.

And you have to think, not as the version of you today, but the *future you*, the you that's five years ahead, crushing it.

The you who already figured this out, scaled the business, and reclaimed your time and energy.

That's the person you need to take advice from.

The 3 Stages of AI Reinvention

Now, if you're wondering "what does the actual journey look like?" Don't worry, I've got a map for you. Every business, every entrepreneur who successfully brings AI into their world follows three simple stages:

Assist → Augment → Automate.

Think of it like climbing a mountain. You don't leap to the summit; you take it step by step.

Stage 1: Assist

This is where most people start, and it's a fantastic place to be.

Imagine AI as your personal assistant who never sleeps, never gets tired, and doesn't need coffee breaks. At this stage, you're using AI to save time and knock out all that busywork.

Real-world examples

- Drafting emails in half the time
- Brainstorming social media posts in minutes
- Researching blog topics without falling down a 6-hour Google rabbit hole

Sarah's AI Transformation: From 3 Hours to 20 Minutes

Let's take Sara, for example, a busy leadership coach with a thriving practice, who used to spend two to three hours writing a single blog post. She'd sit at her computer, staring at a blank screen, wrestling with writer's block, second-guessing every sentence, and constantly deleting and rewriting paragraphs. By the time she finished, she was mentally exhausted and often questioned whether her content was even good enough to publish.

After learning to use AI at the "assist" stage, she cut her blog writing time down to just 20 minutes, and the content was *better* than what she was writing before.

Sarah's Step-by-Step AI Blog Writing Process

Here's exactly how Sarah transformed her content creation process:

Step 1: The Brain Dump (2 minutes)

Instead of starting with a blank page, Sarah learned to do a quick "brain dump" with AI. She would open her AI assistant and say:

> *"I want to write a blog post about leadership challenges for new managers. Here are some random thoughts: imposter syndrome, delegation difficulties, giving feedback, team dynamics, and setting boundaries. Help me organize these into a coherent blog post structure."*

The AI would immediately provide her with a structured outline, complete with subheadings and logical flow. No more staring at blank screens.

Step 2: The Content Sprint (10 minutes)

With her outline in hand, Sarah would work section by section with AI:

> *"Write an engaging introduction for my blog post about new manager challenges. My audience is mid-level professionals who have just been promoted. Make it relatable and include a story about feeling overwhelmed in the first week."*

The AI would generate content that Sarah could immediately see, edit, and refine. She'd then prompt for each section:

> *"Now write the section on delegation challenges. Include why new managers struggle to let go of tasks and provide 2-3 practical tips for gradual delegation."*

Step 3: The Personal Touch (5 minutes)

This was Sarah's secret sauce. She never used AI content verbatim. Instead, she'd take the AI-generated draft and add her personal stories, client examples (anonymized), and unique insights. She'd ask herself:

- "What story from my coaching practice illustrates this point?"
- "What would I tell my clients about this?"
- "How can I make this more authentically 'me'?"

Step 4: The Polish Pass (3 minutes)

Finally, Sarah would do a quick review with AI:

> *"Review this blog post for clarity, engagement, and flow. Suggest any improvements to make it more compelling for leadership coaches' audiences."*

The Results Were Remarkable

Before AI: Sarah's content creation process was a source of constant stress and frustration. Each blog post consumed two to three hours of her precious time, often stretching into her evenings and weekends. She battled frequent writer's block, sitting paralyzed in front of her computer screen, and experienced high levels of anxiety every time she needed to create content. Her posting schedule was inconsistent at best, with weeks sometimes passing between publications, and she constantly doubted whether her content was good enough to share with her audience.

After AI: The transformation was nothing short of remarkable. Sarah's blog writing time plummeted to just twenty minutes per post, allowing her to maintain a calm, efficient process that actually energized rather than drained her. She began posting consistently every week, never missing her self-imposed deadlines. Most surprisingly, her engagement rates increased significantly, with readers responding to her content more enthusiastically than ever before. Perhaps most importantly, she developed genuine confidence in her expertise and her ability to communicate it effectively to her audience.

The Bigger Picture

Sarah's transformation wasn't just about saving time (though those extra 2.5 hours per week added up to over 100 hours per year). It was about removing the friction that was keeping her from sharing her expertise with the world. She went from dreading content creation to actually looking forward to it.

Within three months of implementing this AI-assisted approach, Sarah had:

- Published 24 consistent blog posts (vs. eight sporadic posts the previous year)
- Increased her email list by 300%
- Attracted 12 new premium coaching clients
- Been invited as a guest on five podcasts

The real magic wasn't in the technology; it was in how the technology freed Sarah to focus on what she did best: being an exceptional leadership coach with valuable insights to share.

Bottom line:

At the "Assist" stage, you're still doing the work, but AI is your secret superpower, enabling you to move faster and smarter.

Stage 2: Augment

This is where the magic truly begins to happen. At Stage 2, AI isn't just helping you do what you *already* do; it's expanding what's *possible*.

Here's what shifts: You stop thinking of AI like a digital assistant, and you start treating it like a business partner. You begin creating custom AI models based on your expertise, designing frameworks and systems that AI can run instead of you doing everything manually, and letting AI co-create your content, your marketing plans, and your customer service scripts.

Tom's AI Clone: From Overwhelmed Expert to Strategic CEO

Let's give you another example. Tom is a seasoned executive coach with an incredible reputation built over fifteen years. He had a huge body of knowledge, a waiting list of corporate clients, and speaking engagements booked months in advance. There was just one problem: Tom was drowning in his own success. He was working 70-hour weeks, had no time for strategic thinking, and was turning down lucrative opportunities because he simply couldn't clone himself.

That's when we decided to create Tom's "AI clone", and the transformation was nothing short of extraordinary.

Step 1: The Knowledge Harvest (Week 1)

Tom's first step was gathering his intellectual property. Over the course of a week, he collected fifteen years of content: his keynote presentations, workshop materials, blog posts, coaching frameworks, client case studies (anonymized), video transcripts, and even audio recordings from his coaching sessions (with permission).

We uploaded everything into a custom AI training system. The volume was staggering: over 500,000 words of Tom's expertise, methodologies, and unique insights. However, this wasn't just about quantity; we organized the content by theme, coaching methodologies, and client types to ensure the AI could understand the context and nuances of Tom's approach.

Step 2: Teaching the AI to "Think" Like Tom (Week 2)

This was the most crucial phase. We didn't just dump information into the AI; we taught it Tom's decision-making patterns, his coaching style, and his communication voice. Tom spent hours providing the AI with examples:

> *"When a client says they're struggling with team dynamics, here's how I typically respond..." "My framework for leadership development follows these five stages..." "When I'm writing for C-suite executives versus middle managers, here's how my tone shifts..."*

We created what we called "Tom's Mental Models", detailed prompts that captured his coaching philosophy, his preferred frameworks, and even his sense of humor.

Step 3: The Testing Phase (Week 3)

Before releasing the AI, we conducted extensive tests. Tom would present real client scenarios to his AI clone and compare the responses to how he would actually handle them. Initially, the AI was about 60% accurate. But as we refined the training and added more specific examples, that accuracy jumped to over 90%.

Tom was amazed when the AI clone suggested a coaching intervention he had literally used with a similar client just two weeks earlier.

Step 4: Deployment and Integration (Week 4 onwards)

Once Tom trusted his AI clone, we integrated it into his daily workflow:

Keynote Speech Drafting: Tom would give his AI clone the event details, audience demographics, and key message. Within minutes, he'd receive a complete 30-minute speech draft in his voice, complete with his signature stories and frameworks. What used to take him 8-10 hours now took 45 minutes of review and personalization.

Client Session Preparation: Before coaching sessions, Tom would brief his AI clone on the client's background and challenges. The AI would suggest specific coaching questions, recommend relevant frameworks, and even anticipate potential areas of resistance. Tom's session prep time dropped from 45 minutes to 10 minutes per client.

Content Creation: The AI clone could write blog posts, LinkedIn articles, and even email newsletters that sounded authentically like Tom. He'd provide a topic and key points, and receive publication-ready content that required minimal editing.

Proposal Writing: When potential clients requested custom proposals, Tom's AI clone could draft comprehensive responses based on similar past engagements, complete with pricing, methodology, and outcome projections.

Step 5: The Continuous Learning Loop

The most powerful aspect of Tom's AI clone was its ability to learn and improve. Every week, Tom would review the AI's outputs, provide feedback, and add new insights. The AI clone became more sophisticated over time, learning Tom's preferences and refining its responses.

The Results Were Life-Changing

Before the AI Clone: Tom was working 70-hour weeks, constantly stressed about keeping up with demand. He was turning down speaking engagements and new clients because he didn't have capacity. His content creation had become sporadic, and he felt like he was always playing catch-up. Despite his success, he was seriously considering scaling back his business because the workload was unsustainable.

After the AI Clone: Tom reclaimed 20 hours per week while maintaining the same level of output quality, in many cases, improving it. He could now accept speaking engagements that he would have previously declined, take on additional coaching clients, and still have time for strategic business development. His content production increased by 300%, and he launched two new digital courses because he finally had the bandwidth to focus on scaling his expertise.

The Bigger Business Impact

Within six months of deploying his AI clone, Tom had:

- Increased his revenue by 150% without increasing his working hours
- Launched two passive income digital courses
- Accepted 12 additional speaking engagements
- Taken on eight new premium coaching clients
- Published 48 pieces of high-quality content (vs. 12 the previous year)
- Developed a scalable system that he could eventually license to other coaches

Bottom line: Stage 2 is where you transition from a worker bee to a CEO. You're no longer just working *in* your business; you're building a machine that works *for* your business. Tom didn't just get his time back; he created a sustainable, scalable model that turned his expertise into a systematic competitive advantage.

Stage 3: Automate

And here's the top of the mountain. At Stage 3, you **step out of the weeds completely.** You become the *architect* of the business, not the operator.

AI, smart systems, and automation now handle marketing and lead generation, sales conversations with AI-enhanced touchpoints, client onboarding and delivery, content creation and publishing, as well as analytics and decision support.

Picture this: You wake up in the morning, open your dashboard, and see leads coming in, content being published, clients being served, and sales being made **WITHOUT you touching a thing.**

That's not a fantasy. It's the real future if you commit to building the systems now.

[Case Study Example Client]
Jessica's Automated Empire: The Business That Runs Itself

One more example to help you see how this could work for you. Jessica was a successful business consultant making mid-six figures, but she was trapped in what she called "the success prison." Every dollar she earned required her direct involvement. She couldn't take a vacation without her revenue stopping. She couldn't scale beyond her personal capacity. Despite her expertise and reputation, she was essentially running the world's most expensive job.

Fast forward just a year later, Jessica is sitting on the beach in Santorini. She is holding a cocktail in one hand and her phone in the other, showing her business dashboard. The message reads: *"$47,000 in new sales this week."* She has not spoken to a single prospect. The business is literally running itself. Here's exactly how Jessica built her automated empire, step by step.

Phase 1: The Foundation Assessment (Month 1)

Jessica's transformation began with a brutal audit of every task in her business. We tracked her time for 30 days and categorized every activity into four buckets: Strategic Thinking, Client Delivery, Business

Operations, and Administrative Tasks. The results were shocking: Jessica was spending only 20% of her time on strategic thinking and actual consulting work. The other 80% was consumed by tasks that could theoretically be systematized.

We mapped out her entire customer journey, from initial awareness to ongoing client relationships. Every touchpoint, every email, every conversation was documented. This wasn't glamorous work, but it was essential. You can't automate what you haven't first systematized.

Phase 2: The Content Engine (Months 2-3)

Building on the AI clone concept from Stage 2, Jessica created what we called her "Content Factory." But this wasn't just about generating content; it was about creating an entire ecosystem that worked around the clock.

The Automated Content Calendar: Using AI and smart scheduling tools, Jessica's system generated topic ideas based on trending industry keywords, seasonal business cycles, and her audience's engagement patterns. Every Monday, the system would analyze the previous week's content performance and automatically adjust the upcoming week's content strategy.

Multi-Platform Publishing: Jessica's AI clone would create a single piece of core content, then automatically adapt it for LinkedIn articles, Twitter threads, blog posts, email newsletters, and even short video scripts. One 30-minute content planning session with Jessica would provide her marketing team with content for an entire month.

Engagement Automation: Smart AI tools monitored her social media mentions, comments, and direct messages. The system could handle 80% of routine interactions automatically, only flagging complex questions or high-value prospects for Jessica's personal attention.

Phase 3: The Lead Generation Machine (Months 4-5)

This is where Jessica's business transformation became truly remarkable. She built what she called her "Prospect Magnet", a sophisticated lead generation system that attracted, qualified, and nurtured prospects without her involvement.

The Educational Funnel: Jessica created a comprehensive lead magnet (a business optimization assessment tool) that automatically collected detailed information about prospects' challenges, goals, and budgets. But here's the genius part: the tool provided immediate value by giving prospects a customized action plan, positioning Jessica as the expert before they ever spoke to her.

AI-Powered Lead Scoring: The system analyzed every interaction, website visit, email open, and content engagement to automatically score leads. High-scoring prospects were immediately routed to Jessica's calendar for discovery calls. Medium-scoring prospects entered nurture sequences. Low-scoring prospects received valuable content to build the relationship over time.

Smart Retargeting: Jessica's system tracked prospect behavior across multiple platforms and automatically created custom audiences for targeted advertising. If someone downloaded her assessment but didn't book a call, they'd see her case study ads on LinkedIn. If they visited her pricing page but didn't purchase, they'd receive email testimonials from similar clients.

Phase 4: The Sales Automation Revolution (Months 6-7)

Jessica's most ambitious automation project was systemizing her sales process. This required careful balance, maintaining the personal touch that closed high-value deals while automating everything else.

The Pre-Qualified Discovery Process: By the time prospects reached Jessica's calendar, they had already provided detailed information about their challenges, timeline, and budget through her automated assessment tools. Her AI system prepared customized discovery call agendas, identified the most relevant case studies to reference, and even suggested pricing strategies based on similar past clients.

Automated Proposal Generation: After discovery calls, Jessica's AI clone could generate comprehensive proposals in minutes. The system accessed her database of past projects, pricing models, and outcome metrics to create customized proposals that felt completely personalized. What used to take Jessica 3-4 hours now takes 15 minutes of review and customization.

Follow-Up Sequences: The system managed all follow-up communications, sending the right message at the right time based on prospect behavior. If someone opens the proposal but doesn't respond, they will receive social proof case studies. If they asked about pricing, they'd get financing options and ROI calculators.

Phase 5: Client Delivery Automation (Months 8-10)

The final piece of Jessica's automated empire was systematizing client delivery without sacrificing quality.

Automated Onboarding: New clients entered a sophisticated onboarding sequence that collected all necessary information, set expectations, and provided initial assessments, all before their first official session with Jessica. Clients felt incredibly well-served, as Jessica saved them hours of administrative time.

Intelligent Session Management: Jessica's system scheduled sessions based on optimal timing algorithms, automatically sent preparation materials and agendas, and even provided post-session summaries and action items. Her role shifted from administrative coordinator to strategic advisor.

Progress Tracking and Reporting: Automated systems tracked client progress against their goals, sent regular updates to stakeholders, and flagged accounts that needed additional attention. Jessica could focus on strategic coaching while automation handled accountability and progress management.

Phase 6: The Intelligence Layer (Months 11-12)

The final phase was building what Jessica called her "Business Intelligence Command Center", a dashboard that gave her complete visibility into every aspect of her automated business.

Predictive Analytics: The system analyzed patterns in lead generation, sales cycles, and client outcomes to predict future performance. Jessica could see three months ahead which marketing channels would be most effective, which months would be strongest for sales, and which clients might need additional support.

Automated Optimization: Perhaps most impressively, Jessica's system continuously optimized itself. If email subject lines with certain keywords performed better, the system would automatically adjust future campaigns. If prospects from specific industries had higher conversion rates, ad spend would automatically shift toward those audiences.

The Transformation Results

Before Automation: Jessica was working 60-hour weeks, personally involved in every aspect of her business. She couldn't take vacations without revenue stopping. Her income was directly tied to the number of available hours she had. She was turning down opportunities because she couldn't handle the workload. Despite her success, she felt like she was running in place.

After Automation: Jessica now works 25 hours per week while generating 300% more revenue than her pre-automation peak. Her business runs profitably even when she's traveling for weeks at a time. She's scaled from a solo consultant to running a consulting firm with multiple revenue streams. Most importantly, she's reclaimed her life while exponentially increasing her impact.

The Compound Effect

Eighteen months after completing her automation journey, Jessica's business had evolved into something unprecedented. She was generating seven figures annually while working fewer hours than most part-time employees. Her automated systems had identified and captured opportunities she never could have managed manually. She'd launched two additional revenue streams (online courses and certification programs) that required minimal ongoing involvement but generated substantial passive income.

Most remarkably, Jessica had begun licensing her automation frameworks to other consultants, creating a meta-business that helped others achieve similar transformations. Her "success prison" had become a freedom empire, and she was helping others break free from the same constraints that had once trapped her.

Picture this: You wake up in the morning, open your dashboard, and see leads coming in, content being published, clients being served, and sales being made **WITHOUT you touching a thing.** That's not a fantasy. It's Jessica's reality, and it can be yours too if you commit to building the systems now.

The Goal: Move from Assist to Automate in 6-12 Months

This isn't a "maybe someday" project.

To stay competitive, you need to progress through these stages **within the next year.**

Why?

Because the old way of doing business, the way where success is tied to how many hours you grind, is disappearing fast.

The businesses that survive and thrive will be the ones that own intelligent, self-operating ecosystems.

You're not competing against other people anymore. You're competing against systems.

The AI Reinvention Roadmap: Step-by-Step

Here's your easy roadmap to move from "I'm interested" to "I'm unstoppable."

Month 1: Foundation

- Audit your current time-wasters.
- Set up basic AI helpers.
- Create your first prompt templates.
- Start documenting your secret sauce (your frameworks and IP).

Month 2: Augmentation

- Build your first custom AI trained on *you.*
- Set up simple automations.
- Multiply your content effortlessly.
- Create your first AI-powered lead magnet or quiz.

Month 3: Authority Building

- Launch your AI-fueled content machine.
- Install advanced analytics.
- Start mapping out your authority book (yes, you're writing a book, I'll show you how!)
- Create your first AI-enhanced lead nurture funnel.

Months 4-6: Advanced Growth

- Finish your book or signature authority asset.
- Build automated client acquisition systems.
- Launch AI-enhanced client delivery systems.

- Implement decision frameworks to make smarter choices more quickly.

Case Study: The Complete AI Business Transformation,

Let's call him Dr. T. He had built an incredibly successful medical practice. Yet like many busy experts, he faced a familiar challenge: turning his deep expertise into greater visibility, broader reach, and scalable growth. Between managing patients and running his practice, finding time to write a book, create content, or expand his brand seemed impossible.

That changed when he started strategically leveraging AI. The first step was to create a comprehensive Ideal Customer Profile, utilizing AI to thoroughly analyze the audience, messaging, and digital presence. From there, AI tools helped rapidly map out an entire book based on his ideas, experiences, and expertise —a project that would have taken months to complete manually, now accomplished in just days.

Beyond the book, Dr. T. utilized AI to create a comprehensive library of patient education materials, blog posts, social media content, and marketing assets, all perfectly aligned with his voice and brand. But the reinvention didn't stop with marketing. By integrating AI into his business processes, he streamlined lead generation, improved client onboarding, and set up intelligent systems for consistent patient communication and follow-up, freeing him from hours of administrative work.

Within weeks, Dr. T. had a complete brand refresh, new marketing systems running, and an expanded platform for reaching both patients and professional networks. He boosted his visibility, secured new speaking opportunities, and positioned himself as the top thought leader in his field, all while gaining back valuable time to focus on what he does best.

By embracing AI not just as a content creator but as a business partner, Dr. T. not only saved time but also leveraged it to drive business growth. He built a smarter, stronger, and fully scalable business foundation for the future.

This wasn't just an evolution, it was a reinvention.

Achieving AI Mastery

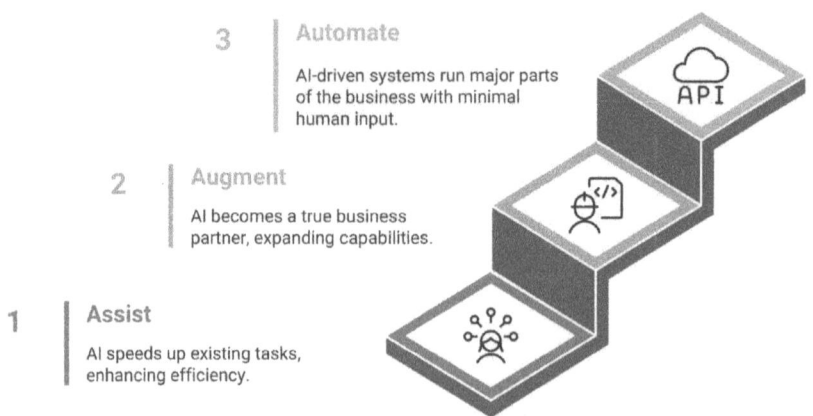

3	**Automate**
	AI-driven systems run major parts of the business with minimal human input.
2	**Augment**
	AI becomes a true business partner, expanding capabilities.
1	**Assist**
	AI speeds up existing tasks, enhancing efficiency.

Summary

In a world of constant change, future-proofing your business isn't about guessing what's next; it's about preparing for a range of possibilities. The path to AI mastery follows three clear stages: **Assist**, where AI speeds up your existing tasks; **Augment**, where AI becomes a true business partner expanding your capabilities; and **Automate**, where AI-driven systems run major parts of your business with minimal human input. The goal is to move from Assist to Automate within 6 to 12 months. By following a structured AI Reinvention Roadmap, entrepreneurs can dramatically increase efficiency, reclaim time, grow visibility, and create self-sustaining authority platforms that lead their industries instead of chasing them. The future doesn't wait; it rewards those who build it today.

Action Steps

1. **Identify which stage of AI Reinvention you are currently in:** Assist, Augment, or Automate.

2. **Conduct an audit** of your daily business activities and highlight tasks that can be accelerated or automated with AI.

3. **Create basic AI helpers:** set up tools for writing, research, and content generation to support your workflow.

4. **Begin training a custom AI** model using your existing content, such as talks, blogs, videos, or webinars.

5. **Launch your first AI-supported lead generation asset** (such as a quiz, assessment, or free guide).

6. **Develop a clear timeline over the next 6 to 12 months** to move from manual tasks to a fully automated business ecosystem.

CHAPTER 12

MAKING THE LEAP, YOUR 90-DAY TRANSFORMATION PLAN

The future depends on what you do today.

–Mahatma Gandhi

Alright, you've been soaking up the strategies, the frameworks, and the examples.

And right about now, you're probably thinking, *"Okay, this all sounds amazing, but can I really pull this off?"*

The answer is simple: **YES. YOU. CAN.**

But there's a little secret I have to tell you:

Knowledge alone doesn't change your life.

Action does.

You don't get transformation from reading a book.

You get transformation by doing the bold, scary, exciting things that most people will *only* dream about. It's when you take that leap, even when it's uncomfortable, even when you're not sure how it's all going to turn out. That's how Jenn and I roll. We don't wait around for perfect timing or everything to line up just right. We move. We act. And that's exactly how our publishing company was born.

We were at a marketing conference in San Diego, between sessions and literally on our breaks, when the idea came to us. Instead of tucking it away for "someday," we whipped out our phones and shot the landing page videos right then and there. We brainstormed the name, created the logo, and started building the vision, all from a spark of inspiration and a whole lot of action. That's the kind of energy you want to bring to the table. You've got to take that first step, even if it's a messy one, because that's where the magic happens.

Let's make it simple, doable, and realistic.

I'm handing you a 90-day plan to reinvent your business, and your future, starting today.

Are you ready? (I know you are. Let's go!)

The 90-Day Reinvention Challenge

This isn't just another "goal-setting exercise."

This is a line-in-the-sand, "I'm done playing small" kind of moment.

Here's what you're going to do in the next 90 days:

1. **Publish your book** (or at least your bold manifesto, your statement to the world)
2. **Build your AI-powered Authority Engine** (yes, we're building your *machine*)
3. **Close 3+ high-ticket clients** using your new platform
4. **Launch your Signature Platform** (your talk, your framework, your offer)

Big? Yes.

Bold? Absolutely.

Possible? 1000%, if you commit and follow the steps.

The Identity Shift: You 2.0

Let's get real for a minute:

You're not just building better systems.
You're not just automating a few processes.

You are building a whole new version of YOU.

A YOU who thinks in leverage, not labor.
A YOU who focuses on vision, not just operations.
A YOU who leads, not chases.

This is personal. This is leadership. This is legacy.

You can't future-proof your business if you're stuck in yesterday's identity.

You've got to *become* the founder your future business needs.

The Truth About Transformation

And here's the honest part no one likes to talk about: **Before you can build, you have to burn.** Burn the old offers that no longer light you up. Burn the habits that keep you in "busy" mode instead of "builder" mode. Burn the fear that tells you "maybe later" or "what if it doesn't work?" When you reinvent, you're not just adding new things; you're *making space* by subtracting the stuff that's weighing you down.

Transformation isn't always pretty. Over the last decade or so, Jenn and I have seen it all: the highs, the wins, the tears, the late nights, and the moments when quitting felt easier. But we kept showing up. We've helped hundreds of authors go from idea to bestseller, and the truth is, it's never a straight line. Real transformation comes with messy drafts, doubts, and doing the hard stuff when no one's clapping for you. But if you stay the course, just like we have, through pivots, reinventions, and bold leaps, you end up not just with a book, but a brand, a business, and a life that looks completely different than where you started. That's the truth about transformation.

Ask yourself:

- What am I DONE tolerating?
- What must die for my next level to be born?
- What version of me needs to step aside so the next version can rise?

It's deep work, but it's the *only* way to rise.

Shift From Operator to Architect

Let me paint you a picture: **Operators** are always hustling. They're buried in tasks. They're reacting, not creating.

Architects, on the other hand? They *design* systems. They *build* brands that work while they sleep. They *own* assets instead of selling hours.

Over the next 90 days, your mission is to shift from being the operator in your business to being the *architect*. You're not just building a business. You're building a machine. You're building an empire. You're building your freedom.

Your 90-Day Action Plan

Let's break it down:

Days 1–30: Foundation Phase

This is your "planting seeds" phase.

1. **Define Your "Category of One" Positioning**

   You're not just another coach, consultant, creative, or CEO. You are unique. You need to own a category, a space no one else can claim.

   What's the big problem you solve?
   Why are YOU the obvious solution?
   What's your core message that no one else can say?

2. **Document Your Frameworks and Methodologies**

   Your magic isn't random. It's a process. It's a method. Document it!

   (Tip: Record yourself teaching or coaching, then use AI to turn it into a framework.)

3. **Set Up Your Initial AI Tools**

   Get your Tech Stack locked in: GPTs, automations, content systems.

4. **Start Developing Your Book or Manifesto**

   Even if you're terrified, start. A book isn't about being a "writer." It's about being a **leader** with something to say.

Days 31–60: Authority Building Phase

Now, we turn your ideas into a platform.

1. **Complete Your Book Draft or Manifesto**

   (Hint: You don't have to be perfect. You just have to be published.)

2. **Build Your Content Multiplication System**

   AI can turn one blog into 20 LinkedIn posts, 10 tweets, and five emails, without you lifting a finger.

3. **Create Your High-Ticket Offer Structure**

   Design an irresistible, transformational offer that people *want* to buy. (If you need help here, trust me, this is something we help our clients with every day.)

4. **Implement Lead Generation Assets**

   Launch that quiz, that assessment, that AI-automated lead magnet. Build a list of people who actually *want* what you're about to offer.

Days 61–90: Monetization Phase

This is GO TIME.

1. **Launch Your Authority Book or Manifesto**

   No more hiding. No more waiting. Publish and promote.

2. **Activate Your Content Ecosystem**

   Your AI systems should now be dripping out content daily, like your own marketing team on autopilot.

3. **Outreach to High-Value Prospects**

   Start conversations. Book calls. Make offers.

4. Close Your First High-Ticket Clients

And yes, raise your prices. You are not for everyone. You are for the best.

The Be Recognized Framework in Action

Here's the good news: You don't have to do this alone. We've built something called the **AI Authority Engine**, a full, 90-day "done-with-you" system that walks you through this entire transformation step-by-step.

Here's what you get:

Thought Leadership Extraction & Messaging Clarity

We help you pull out your brilliance and turn it into frameworks, keynotes, books, and authority assets.

Book Content Development

Not sure how to turn your ideas into a book? We'll show you how to get it done, fast, and make it profitable from Day 1.

Fractional AI Officer Strategy

We set up your AI systems, optimize your workflows, and show you how to work less *and* grow faster.

Custom GPTs for Content & Outreach Imagine having your own brand-trained AI that writes your blogs, posts, and emails while you focus on your genius work.

Done-for-You Podcast Pitch Automation

Want to get interviewed, featured, and seen everywhere? We build your pitch system so you don't have to.

Digital Authority Management

We help you dominate AI-driven search engines, build a strong online footprint, and stay relevant long after the buzz fades.

Final Word: This Is Your Moment

Listen, the old game is dead.
The hustle game? Done.
The "just work harder" model? Over.

You're standing at the edge of a brand-new playing field, one where **authority** is everything, and **AI** is the new gatekeeper.

The question is:

Will you sit back and watch others rise?
Or will you build the platform they'll be chasing?

The world doesn't need another "hard worker."
The world needs leaders. Builders. Architects.

It needs **you**.

Be Recognized. Be Remembered. Be Unstoppable.

The future is already here, and it's waiting for you to claim it.

Let's go.

Your Next Steps: Quick-Start Checklist

Alright, you've read the stories.
You've seen the strategy.
You're fired up (I can feel it!).

Now it's time to *turn that spark into action* and become the unstoppable, undeniable authority you're meant to be.

Here's your simple, no-excuses action plan:

1. Choose Your Identity

Decide today to stop being the operator and step fully into being the *architect* of your future business.

2. Audit Your Time

Where are you still stuck doing busywork?
Make a list. That's your starting point for AI and automation.

3. Build Your Tech Stack

Set up your core tools:

- Claude or ChatGPT for brainstorming
- Gamma.app for pitches and decks
- NotebookLM to store and organize your genius
- Descript/RunwayML for fast media creation
- Make.com or Zapier to automate workflows
- Tally/Typeform for smart lead-gen

4. Launch Your Authority Platform

- Start writing your book or manifesto (even if it's messy!)
- Begin posting AI-enhanced content consistently
- Design your high-ticket offer

5. Implement Your 90-Day Plan

Break it into phases:

- Days   1–30: Lay your foundation
- Days 31–60: Build your authority
- Days 61–90: Monetize like a boss

6. *Kill What's Holding You Back*

Old offers, old fears, old ways of thinking, *let them go.*
Make room for your next-level self.

7. *Focus on ONE Big Move Every Week*

Small, consistent action > big, overwhelming plans.
Select one move each week and execute it with confidence.

8. *Build Your Engine, Not Just Your Effort*

If you have to *work harder* to grow, you're building the wrong thing.
Focus on systems. Focus on assets. Focus on multiplication.

9. *Stay Connected to Possibility*

Every day, ask yourself:

> *"How can this be easier?"*
> *"How can this be bigger?"*
> *"How can I make this more fun?"*

10. *Be Recognized. Be Remembered. Be Unstoppable.*

Own your space. Own your voice.
Publish. Show up. Lead.
Your future clients and your future self are waiting for you.

You don't need another year of "getting ready."
You don't need another certification or course.
You don't need permission.

You are ready NOW.
The tools are ready NOW.
The world is ready for you NOW.

Start messy.
Start scared.

Start imperfect.

But for goodness' sake, start.

Your future self is already clapping and cheering you on.

Let's go build the future you deserve.

Summary

Transformation doesn't happen through information alone; it happens through action. In this chapter, you are challenged to move beyond learning into execution. The next 90 days present an opportunity to reinvent your business, brand, and yourself by building systems, establishing your authority platform, attracting premium clients, and transitioning from being an operator to becoming an architect of your future. Success belongs to those who commit boldly, embrace leverage, and build engines that run smarter, faster, and bigger than they ever could alone. Your future isn't something you wait for; it's something you create.

AI-Driven Business Transformation Roadmap

Action Items

1. Define your "Category of One" positioning to own your unique space in the market.

2. Document your core frameworks, IP, and signature methods using simple recording or transcription tools.

3. Set up your initial AI tech stack (writing, automations, content management).

4. Start drafting your book, manifesto, or authority-building asset immediately.

5. Build your high-ticket offer and map out a lead generation plan using AI-enhanced systems.

6. Launch your first batch of AI-supported content across social media, email, and podcasts.

7. Focus each week on executing one major move toward your 90-day milestones.

8. Eliminate old offers, habits, or mindsets that no longer align with the next version of your business.

9. Build and automate your content and outreach engine for sustained growth.

10. Step fully into your role as architect, lead, publish, dominate, and own your authority.

THE FUTURE BELONGS
TO THE BOLD,
SO STEP UP,
STAND OUT,
AND LEAD!

AI TOOLS

App Name	Function	Pillar	URL
Delphi	AI Clone	Connecting, Building	Delphiclone.com
NarrativeBI	Analytics	Investigating	https://narrative.bi
Akkio	analytics	Investigating	Akkio.com
ElevenLabs	Audio	Building	elevenlabs
Zapier	Automation	Streamlining	Zapier.com
Make	Automation	Streamlining	Make.com
MovableType	Book Writing	Building	MovableType.ai
Booksoft	Book Writing	Building	booksoft.ai
VoiceFlow	Bot Builder	Connecting	https://www.voice-flow.com/
Manychat	Bot Builder	Connecting	Manychat.com
Closebot	Bot Builder	Streamlining	Closebot.com
Claude	Chat	Brainstorm-ing, Building, Investigating	claude.ai
Gemini	Chat	Brainstorm-ing, Building, Investigating	https://gemini.google.com
Perplexity	Chat	Brainstorm-ing, Building, Investigating	perplexity.ai
Chathub	Chat	Brainstorming, Building	chathub.gg

ChatGPT	Chat	Brainstorming, Building, Streamlining, Investigating	Chatgpt.com
Google Notebook	Chat	Brainstorming, Building	Notebooklm.google.com
BNSN	Copywriting	Building	BNSN.ai
Gohighlevel	CRM	Streamlining	Gohighlevel.com
Castmagic	Derivative Text Content	Building	castmagic.io
Ready to Send	Email	Streamlining	Getreadytosend.com
Fyxer	Email	Streamlining	fyxer.com
Canva	Graphics	Building	Canva.com
Midjourney	Graphics	Building	Midjourney.com
Flux	Graphics	Building	Flux.ai
Fireflies	Meeting Notes	Investigating, Building	Fireflies.ai
Fathom	Meeting Notes	Investigating, Building	Fathom.video
Otter	Meeting Notes	Investigating, Building	Otter.ai
Suno	Music	Building	Suno.com
Udio	Music	Building	Udio.com
Beautiful	Presentations	Building	Beautiful.ai
Gamma	Presentations	Building	Gamma.app
Notion	Productivity	Brainstorming, Building, Streamlining, Investigating	Notion.com
Founderpal	Strategy	Brainstorming, Building	Founderpal.ai

Waxwing	Strategy	Brainstorming	waxwing.ai
MacWhisper	Transcription	Investigating	https://goodsnooze.gumroad.com/l/macwhisper
HeyGen	Video creation	Building	Heygen.com
synthesia	Video creation	Building	https://www.synthesia.io
Invideo	Video creation	Building	ai.invidio.io
Videogen	Video creation	Building	videogen.io
RunwayML	Video creation	Building	Runwayml.com
Aivideo	Video creation	Building	Aivideo.com
FocalML	Video creation	Building	Focalml.com
Minvo	Video Shorts	Building	minvo.pro
Opus Pro	Video Shorts	Building	opus.pro
Thoughtly	Voice AI	Connecting	Thought.ly
The Oasis	Voice notes	Building	Theoasis.com
Relume	Website Wireframe	Building	Relume.io
Zipwp	Wordpress Creator	Building	Zipwp.com
Writesonic	Writing	Building	Writesonic.com
Wordtune	Writing	Building	Wordtune.com
CreatorBuddy	Writing	Building	creatorbuddy.io/?via=start
Taplio	Writing	Building	Taplio.com
Genspark	Chat, Agentic	Building, Streamlining, Brainstorming, Connecting, Investigating	https://Genspark.vip

| Manus | Chat, Agentic | Brainstorming, Building, Connecting, Investigating, Streamlining | https://go.accelerated intelligence.ai/tools/ manus |
| Lovable | Vibe Coding | Building | https://go.accelerated intelligence.ai/tools/ lovable |

The Best AI Tools by Category

AI Assistants (Chatbots): ChatGPT, Claude, Gemini, DeepSeek, Grok

Video Generation and Editing: Synthesia, Runway, Filmora, OpusClip

Image Generation: GPT-4o, Midjourney

Diagrams: Napkin.ai

Notetakers and Meeting Assistants: Fathom, Nyota

Research: Deep Research

Writing: Rytr, Sudowrite

Grammar and Writing Improvement: Grammarly, Wordtune

Search Engines: Perplexity, ChatGPT search

Social Media Management: Vista Social, FeedHive

Graphic Design: Canva Magic Studio, Looka

App Builders & Coding: Bubble, Bolt, Lovable, Cursor, v0

Project Management: Asana, ClickUp

Scheduling: Reclaim, Clockwise

Customer Service: Tidio AI, Hiver

Recruitment: Textio, CVViZ

Knowledge Management: Notion AI Q&A, Guru

Email: Hubspot Email Writer, SaneBox, Shortwave

Presentations: Gamma, Presentations.ai

Resume Builders: Teal, Kickresume

Voice Generation: ElevenLabs, Murf

Music Generation: Suno, Udio

Marketing: AdCreative

Sales: Clay

Other AI Tools We Love

- NotebookLM - Turn any content into a podcast in minutes!
- ChatHub GG - Run 6 AI systems at a time: (another one is https://poe.com)
- Suno for creating music in 30 seconds
- HeyGen for video clones
- Otter for real-time transcripts:
- Oasis for rapidly creating content with voice
- Claude (the best AI for writing for copy, HIPAA compliant)
- ChatGPT (the first and best overall): https://chat.openai.com (explore the GPTs)
- CastMagic for creating podcast content in minutes
- Opus for turning long-form into short-form
- Gamma for fast presentation creation: https://gamma.app
- InVideo creates marketing videos in minutes
- VideoGen is like InVideo (faster, not the same quality): https://videogen.io
- Fathom - the best for recording and summarizing Zoom and Google meetings with video

- Delphi for real-time, smart systems that write like you, can do customer support and more (try the demo here). Create your own Delphi Clone here
- IdeoGram (best tool for generating graphics with GOOD SPELLING!)
- MacWhisper (a desktop App that does batch transcripts and more)
- YOUTUBE TOOLS for Quick-Learning:
  - YouTube Transcript Plugin
  - ChatTube (12 free chats per day)
  - Tactiq - rapid transcriptions of YouTube videos that work on mobile devices

Visit BeRecognized.us to get a downloadable PDF of the AI Tools

GET OUR FREE BOOK

Need help writing your book? Download or read the book
Strategic Writing System FREE HERE.

Strategic Writing System

VIP BOOK WRITING DAY

Does this sound like you?

You're ready to get your book out of your brain and into the world.

You're ready to finally finish the book you've been working on.

You wish you had time to just focus (not just an hour or two here and there).

You wish you had someone who has been where you are, who could give you a strategic roadmap.

You value the power of community and crave a connection with other authors.

Sign up for our VIP Book Creation Day

Get an exclusive, one-on-one coaching experience, and you get the personalized attention you deserve to ignite your book project and write the story you've been wanting to share.

Leave our VIP Day with nearly 30% of your book written, plus a framework and formula to finish the rest in less time than you think!

Get the insight, expert planning, and instruction to take your book idea from "I'm stuck" to "Whoo-hoo, I've finally finished my book!"

You won't get this kind of in-depth personalized service anywhere else.

Note: This is NOT a group session. This is a 1:1 session designed specifically for YOU!

Sign up at **EliteOnlinePublishing.com/vip-book-writing-day**

BESTSELLER SOLUTIONS TRAINING COURSE

The number one national bestseller list is the Holy Grail for authors. Getting your book onto that list can mean huge sales and a huge boost to your career. But how do you get there? The answer is marketing. And the best place to start is with the Bestseller Solutions Digital Training Course.

This course will teach you everything you need to know about marketing your book to bestseller status on Amazon. You'll learn how to choose the right category and keywords, how to price your book for maximum impact, and how to create an effective launch strategy. You'll also get access to exclusive resources, like a list of where to speak on stages in your genre and advice from successful authors who have been there before.

If you're serious about making your book a bestseller, the Bestseller Solutions Digital Training Course is essential. Invest in your success today and see the rewards tomorrow.

Visit **BestsellerSolutions.com** for membership access Today.

LISTEN TO OUR PODCASTS

We produce two weekly podcasts designed to grow your business, improve your mindset, and learn the inside secrets to publishing.

ELITE EXPERT INSIDER

The *Elite Expert Insider* podcast was created to educate, inspire, and motivate entrepreneurs, innovators, and growth seekers. Hosts Melanie Johnson and Jenn Foster, owners of Elite Online Publishing, will bring you conversations from business, personal development, to health and fitness. They will chat with special guests, industry leaders, authors, business and marketing experts, and just darn interesting people. It's the show that will up your game!

Listen to the Podcast on iTunes, Spotify, YouTube, or wherever you prefer to listen to podcasts.

ELITE PUBLISHING PODCAST

The *Elite Publishing Podcast* is for inspired writers and authors. If you want to write a book and become a bestselling author, you are in the right place. At Elite Online Publishing, we can help you create, publish, and market your book so that it becomes a #1 bestseller. We work with a limited number of authors to ensure that they receive the best possible service, so if you want to learn how to write and publish a book that will empower you to smartly grow your brand, business, and credibility, listen today.

Listen to the Podcast on iTunes, Spotify, YouTube, Amazon Alexa, or wherever you prefer to listen to podcasts.

SPEAKING

Book Melanie Johnson to Speak

Book Melanie as your keynote speaker and you're guaranteed to make your event inspirational, motivational, highly entertaining, and unforgettable.

Melanie graduated from Michigan State University with a degree in communications and was the first girl to receive a varsity letter in a boys' sport in the state of Michigan.

As a single Mom raising two sons, she knows what it takes to succeed.

For more information and to book Melanie to speak for your next event, visit EliteOnlinePublishing.com/speaking.

Enjoy this special gift. The #1 bestselling Story Starter book from Elite Online Publishing, written by Melanie Johnson and Jenn Foster. *How To Write Your Story of Success to Impact the World: A Story Starter Guide to Write Your Business or Personal Stories, Goals, and Achievements*

Visit **gift.EliteOnlinePublishing.com** to receive
your FREE BOOK.

Visit our YouTube Channel for Tips, Ideas, and More:
YouTube.com/eliteonlinepublishing1

ABOUT THE AUTHORS

Melanie Churella Johnson is a powerhouse media mogul, AI strategist, and publishing expert who is reshaping how entrepreneurs build influence in the digital age. She is the founder and CEO of Elite Online Publishing, a company that has published over 3,000 books—earning all of its authors #1 bestseller status. A trailblazer in media and business, Melanie previously owned and operated two independent television stations in Houston and Dallas, growing them into a $100 million enterprise.

Melanie is the WSJ/USA Today bestselling author of 18 books and a TEDx speaker. Her latest book, *Be Recognized: The AI Authority Engine*, co-authored with Jenn Foster, offers a revolutionary system for turning expertise into scalable authority using artificial intelligence. Through this groundbreaking work, Melanie has become a sought-after voice on how business leaders can future-proof their brands and build legacy platforms with the power of AI.

She is the co-host of two award-winning podcasts, *Elite Expert Insider* and *Elite Publishing Podcast*, and a leading authority on content repurposing, strategic visibility, and smart automation. Her AI-powered marketing and publishing systems have helped hundreds of entrepreneurs dominate their niche, increase revenue, and gain national recognition, without working around the clock.

Beyond publishing, Melanie is known for her real estate ventures, transforming two luxury homes, the 25,000 sq ft Houston Mansion and the 13,000 sq ft Walloon Lake House, into six-figure short-term rental businesses. She also founded Charity Auction Consignments, helping nonprofits raise over $600,000.

A former Miss Michigan and first runner-up to Miss America, Melanie began her career as a news anchor in Detroit. She holds a communications degree from Michigan State University and made history as the first girl in the state to receive a varsity letter in a boys' sport. As a single mother of two sons, she embodies resilience, reinvention, and visionary leadership.

Linkedin.com/in/melaniejohnson-eop/
Instagram.com/melaniecjohnson/
Youtube.com/eliteonlinepublishing1
Linkedin.com/company/elite-online-publishing

Jenn Foster is a trailblazing digital marketing strategist, AI publishing pioneer, and multi-award-winning author who is redefining how thought leaders build brand empires in the digital age. She is the co-author of the bestselling book *Be Recognized: The AI Authority Engine for Experts Who Want to Be Known, Be Profitable, and Be Published*, and the co-founder of Elite Online Publishing, where she has helped thousands of authors reach #1 bestseller status.

A Wall Street Journal, USA Today, and International bestselling author an incredible 18 times over, Jenn combines deep technical mastery with creative brand storytelling to help entrepreneurs and business professionals transform their expertise into powerful, monetizable platforms. Her digital marketing firm, Biz Social Marketing Agency, has helped hundreds of businesses, from local startups to international corporations, dominate search rankings and drive leads using cutting-edge SEO, automation, and AI content strategies.

Before building her media and publishing empire, Jenn founded and scaled a successful retail chain, where she honed the real-world marketing and operations experience that she brings to every client project. Today, she uses AI tools, publishing systems, and high-level marketing strategies to help clients create books, grow authority, and scale revenue with less time and effort.

Jenn is a graduate of Utah State University, an award-winning web designer, and a sought-after keynote speaker. She has shared the stage with luminaries like Loral Langemeier, Lisa Sasevich, Mike Koenigs, and Ed Rush, and was honored as one of "Utah's Thought Leaders" in the innovation-focused book *Innovate Utah*. She has also been featured in *Stand Apart* by Dan Kennedy and was recognized as one of America's Premier Experts®.

As the co-host of the top-rated *Elite Expert Insider* podcast, Jenn continues to elevate conversations around entrepreneurship, publishing, AI integration, and digital visibility. Her roots run deep in entrepreneurship; her grandfather founded Maverik Country Stores, the renowned gas and retail chain still thriving today, and Jenn's lifelong understanding of business systems gives her a unique edge in helping others scale theirs.

A single mom of three, Jenn is passionate about empowering other business owners to create freedom through smart systems and personal brand leverage. When she's not scaling businesses, she's likely outdoors hiking, boating, or traveling with her kids.

Follow Jenn Foster:
AuthorJennFoster.com
Eliteonlinepublishing.com
Facebook.com/authorjennfoster
@jennfosterchic
Instagram.com/eliteonlinepublishing
YouTube.com/elilteonlinepublishing1
LinkedIn.com/in/jennfosterseo
Linkedin.com/company/elite-online-publishing